Eleven Essentials of
Effective Writing

Ann Marie Radaskiewicz

Western Piedmont Community College

HOUGHTON MIFFLIN COMPANY   Boston   New York

To my son, Mark

Senior Sponsoring Editor: Mary Jo Southern
Associate Editor: Jennifer Roderick
Senior Project Editor: Fred Burns
Senior Production/Design Coordinator: Carol Merrigan
Senior Manufacturing Coordinator: Sally Culler
Senior Marketing Manager: Nancy Lyman

Cover Design: Harold Burch, Harold Burch Design, New York
Cover Image: "10" Steve Edson/Photonica

Printed in the U.S.A.

Library of Congress Catalog Card Number: 99-71916

ISBN: 0-395-96112-2

123456789–FFG-03 02 01 00 99

As part of Houghton Mifflin's ongoing
commitment to the environment, this text
has been printed on recycled paper.

Contents

Preface

Eleven Essentials of Effective Writing offers a unique approach to learning composition by defining the essential characteristics that are always present in effective expository writing of any type. These eleven essentials are:

Creativity and Originality

Vivid Language

Clear Sentences

Complete Paragraphs

Coherent Paragraphs

Cohesive Paragraphs

Logical Organization

Interesting Opening

Effective Closing

Confidence and Assertiveness

Sensitivity and Tact

By reducing good writing to a mere eleven essential characteristics, this text should help students remember those qualities so they can compose clear, interesting prose long after completing their English classes.

The practical information in *Eleven Essentials of Effective Writing* transcends the various expository genres and offers students useful advice they can apply to *anything* they write in their academic, personal, and professional lives. It does not emphasize the academic essay; rather, it presents advice about improving all writing, from letters to memos to reports to research papers. Examples from a wide variety of actual student and professional writing demonstrate how each essential trait is present in any type of effective composition.

Each chapter defines a particular essential, offers a variety of examples from different kinds of compositions, and demonstrates how the application of that essential trait improves the writing. Each chapter includes exercises and writing activities that provide students with opportunities to practice incorporating these essential qualities as they compose.

Features

Eleven Essentials of Effective Writing includes six useful features:

- **Exercises** in each chapter give students practice with a particular concept or technique.

- **Suggested Writing Activities** at the end of each chapter provide students with lists of possible composition topics. To reinforce the idea that the essential characteristics apply to *all* writing—not just the essay—each list contains suggested topics for personal, academic, and professional composition.

- **Tips** about writing and the writing process are inserted throughout each chapter.

- **Chapter Summaries** reinforce the major concepts of each chapter.

- **Sample Student Compositions** in the appendix offer a variety of academic, personal, and professional writings that demonstrate the essential traits discussed in the book.

- A **Revision Checklist** on the inside back cover provides students with a tool for evaluating their own or others' compositions.

Organization

Eleven Essentials of Effective Writing differs significantly from other composition textbooks by organizing information about writing in terms of the *essential characteristics* of effective expository prose rather than by steps in the process or by types of compositions (rhetorical modes). This unique approach addresses the limitation of the process method by defining and illustrating the necessary qualities of the finished product. It also addresses the drawbacks of the rhetorical method, which often ignores many types of documents that don't fit neatly into rigid rhetorical types.

It includes eleven chapters, one for each of the essential traits.

Chapter 1, "Creativity and Originality," discusses the role of the right and left brains in the writing process and offers students eleven different techniques for discovering original, creative ideas.

Chapter 2, "Vivid Language," shows students how to make their writing more vivid and interesting by including details, strong verbs, descriptive adjectives, and figurative language.

Chapter 3, "Four Rules for Clear Sentences," demonstrates how to write clear, concise, direct sentences.

Chapters 4, 5, and 6—"Complete Paragraphs," "Coherent Paragraphs," and "Cohesive Paragraphs"—discuss the "3 C's" of effective paragraphs.

Chapter 7, "Organizing Logical Units," explains how to effectively organize ideas.

Chapter 8, "Interesting Openings," discusses effective openings and offers eight different techniques for getting the reader interested.

Chapter 9, "Effective Closings," illustrates five different techniques for composing satisfying endings.

Chapter 10, "Confidence and Assertiveness," discusses the do's and don't's of writing assertive, confident prose.

Chapter 11, "Sensitivity and Tact," presents the do's and don't's of writing with sensitivity to the reader's needs and feelings.

Acknowledgments

I would like to thank several people who offered their help, support, advice, and ideas for this book.

My colleagues at Western Piedmont Community College—especially Dr. Carolyn West, Paul Wardzinski, and Debra Rose—provided constant support and encouragement.

Betty McFarland and Emory Maiden, through the Appalachian Writing Project at Appalachian State University, led me to discover many of the ideas included in this book.

I am also grateful to Dr. Gerald Schiffhorst, my former professor and advisor at the University of Central Florida, for his helpful advice and encouragement.

I also thank several of my students who gave me permission to print their compositions. Marty McNeely, Brenda Wells, Christel Messer,

Brenda Hunt, Lee Vang, Jean McMullin, Luci Sigmon, and Sandra Lail all contributed writings to this text.

I am indebted to the following reviewers for their suggestions for developing this book: Linda Adams, Jefferson Community College (NY); Beverly Butler, Shippensburg University (PA); Evelyn Etheridge, Paine College (GA); Kathleen Rice, Ivy Tech State College (IN); Robert Scattergood (retired), Belmont Technical College (OH); John Silva, LaGuardia Community College, City University of New York; Edna Troiano, Charles County Community College (MD); Deanna Yameen, Quincy College (MA).

My Houghton Mifflin editors, Mary Jo Southern and Jennifer Roderick, enthusiastically embraced this project and offered insightful suggestions for improvement.

My inspiration, though, is my son Mark. This book is dedicated to him.

Ann Marie Radaskiewicz
Western Piedmont Community College

Introduction

Are there such things as "good writing" and "bad writing"? Can we read an article or a book or a letter and pronounce it good or bad? Fundamentally, does all good writing contain certain qualities? Can we examine, understand, and practice these qualities in our own writing?

The answer to all of these questions is YES. We *can* define what good writing is. All good writing, regardless of genre or form, shares several essential characteristics. This book reveals and explains these common characteristics so that no matter what you must compose—business letter, story, critique, essay, memo, or report—your writing will always be effective because it achieves your purpose.

Each chapter in this book will explore a different characteristic and explain how it applies to a variety of different writing situations: academic, professional, and personal. This approach to writing instruction is unique and innovative. While other textbooks focus on how to compose academic essays, this one presents information that you can use to improve *everything* you write in all areas of your life. All of the examples offered come from real writing of all types: published articles and essays, books, letters, memorandums, reports, student essays, and so on. These examples will demonstrate how you can use the same techniques and strategies no matter what you need to write.

Purpose of This Book

This book takes for granted that you already know how to write. As a matter of fact, you probably learned to write back in first and second grades. But when we become adults, most of us would like to produce more polished writing. This book will help you achieve that in two ways. First of all, it will demonstrate the principles and techniques for increasing the sophistication of your writing. Most of us can already write sentences and paragraphs that can communicate ideas tolerably well. But the goal of this book is to show you the ways to communicate your thoughts using a more complex style.

A second goal of this book is to help you become more aware of *what* you're already doing and *why* you're doing it. Good writers learn to select their methods *consciously,* rather than accidentally. For instance, knowing that you're writing in passive voice—and doing it for a specific reason—will result in a clearer, more effective sentence. Increased knowledge about the process and structure of writing will allow you to make informed choices as you compose.

Before You Write

"I know what I want to say, but I just can't seem to find the right words to say it."

Faced with a writing task, you have probably spoken these words before. Though you have a lot of interesting thoughts and opinions about a lot of different subjects, it often seems as though they all suddenly evaporate as soon as you try to write them down. You rummage around in your mind, looking for those perfect words to express your thoughts, but they elude you, hiding in the shadows. You often complete a writing project less than satisfied, certain that you have not communicated your important ideas as well as you would have liked.

If this has been your experience with writing, you're not alone. Many people find composition a frustrating and difficult activity because they "can't find the right words." But does it have to be this way? Is there anything you can do to find those crucial words you need more easily?

Before we answer those questions, it might be helpful to understand why writing often seems like a baffling game of mental hide-and-go-seek.

Writing, of course, begins with ideas. Like most people, you have plenty of ideas on a variety of topics, and these ideas continually appear and disappear in your mind. Everyone has opinions, and everyone has something significant to say about at least one subject. For example, your interest in NASCAR racing may have resulted in the accumulation of a lot of knowledge about the sport, or your personal experience as a single parent might have given you a lot of knowledge about the advantages and disadvantages of that life situation. Similarly, your work experience may have caused you to form definite opinions about the most efficient procedures for getting a job done. You are constantly thinking, acquiring new ideas, and refining other ideas.

From time to time, you will have to record some of your thoughts in writing, usually in response to some need. For instance, your employer might ask you to write a report, your professor might ask you to compose an essay, or you might need to write a letter explaining a billing error on your monthly credit card statement. Occasionally, you might record some of your thoughts simply because you want to, because you feel compelled to share your knowledge or experience with others. For example, you might want to write an article about one of your hobbies or interests. Regardless of your purpose in writing down those thoughts, they are there in your mind, though you may need to spend more time pondering them before you actually put pen to paper. Yet, many people mistakenly believe that their difficulties with writing are due to a lack of ideas.

On the contrary, once you've decided on a topic to write about, the thoughts are there. However, a lot of them are really only half-formed, incomplete, and rather shadowy things. That's why "finding the right words" is often challenging.

Can you remember the last time someone asked for your opinion about a topic you've never discussed before? Though you may have thought about the subject on your own, you probably found that talking about it with someone else clarified your own beliefs and attitudes. That's because the language you choose to communicate your ideas gives form and shape to those ideas that were only half-thoughts before you put them into words. So, whether you're writing an analysis of a poem, a summary of a magazine article, or a memo about a change in procedure, your thoughts will often tend to be rather insubstantial until you put them into language. Once found, though, those words are guaranteed to increase your own, as well as your reader's, understanding of your meaning.

Now back to our earlier question: What can you do to make your conversion of thought to written word an easier process? *Before* you begin your first draft, always complete two important steps. First of all, THINK about your topic extensively before you write. Many inexperienced writers plunge in without taking the time to explore the thoughts in their mind. Then they wonder why they struggle to put words on the blank paper. Instead, set aside some quiet time to ponder what you know and formulate questions about what you'd like to know. As part of this thinking process, TALK about your topic with others. Discussing it will require you to find language for your thoughts. Finding the language during an informal conversation with another person will help provide you with the words you will use later to communicate your ideas in writing.

The second thing you must do before beginning to write is to change your expectations about the writing process. Do not expect the perfect words to come to you the very first time you attempt to convert thought to language. On the contrary, expect to have to choose words, keep some, and throw some back. Even experienced writers have to experiment with different wordings before they finally decide which ones best communicate their meaning. Inexperienced writers who expect their sentences and paragraphs to be flawless the first time will experience frustration when that perfection eludes them.

Of course, deadlines, other obligations, and dislike of the writing task may pressure you into trying to rush through the composition process. But hurrying will usually only increase your frustration. Expect writing to be a slower procedure of arranging and rearranging words until you discover the combinations that best express what you have to say. Just as the artist works with clay, as you write, you will smooth an area here, pinch off a little excess there, and maybe even flatten a lopsided section to begin again.

While You Write

Several techniques can help you compose a document more easily and quickly.

As you write, draw a blank line or leave a large space when you can't think of the right word so you can keep going. If you stop to spend a lot of time agonizing over one specific word or phrase, you're in danger of forgetting your train of thought or losing sight of your overall goal. As you compose your first draft, it's important to get down your general ideas and structure, so just leave some kind of reminder to yourself that you'll need to fill in a gap later. Chances are that when you return to your document later, when your brain isn't pondering the "big picture," the word you couldn't think of will easily come to you, and you can simply insert it into the blank.

As you're writing, if you need a piece of information or an answer to a question, don't stop composing to go get it. At this point, just jot down your question in the margin of your draft and keep writing. You can find the missing fact or detail and insert it later.

Whenever you get stuck and don't know what to write next, reread your last sentence or paragraph. Reviewing what you've already written is often a springboard that will propel you forward to your next point or idea.

Be aware of the advantages and disadvantages of writing your first draft on paper versus typing it into a computer. Composing the draft using a word processing program may speed up the writing process. Because you eliminate a step by not recording all of your thoughts on paper, you may save some time. Many people who have developed their typing skills also find composing on a computer to be less laborious than handwriting their papers because they can type on a keyboard more easily than they can write. On the other hand, many writers believe that writing by hand is an essential part of the creative process. The physical act of forming letters and words with a pen or pencil, they say, connects the writer's mind and body more intimately to his creation.

Some prefer to type a first draft because a written one is just too messy. When you scribble your thoughts quickly onto a page, crossing out sentences and writing over them again as you search for the right words, the resulting draft can indeed be difficult to read. But one benefit of a handwritten draft is that all of your experiments with different ways to word your thoughts remain there on the page. Even if you scratch out a sentence (never erase anything in a first draft!), you can still read and retrieve it later if you need it elsewhere in the paper. Conversely, a deleted portion of a computer-generated first draft is gone forever. Of course, one way to overcome this drawback is to stop "erasing" your experiments on the screen. Get in the habit of striking (drawing a line) through anything you don't want just as you would on paper. Then those words will still be available if you need them later.

One final disadvantage of a computer-generated draft, especially one produced by a high quality laser printer, is its finished appearance. It's neatly typed and attractive, so the writer might be tempted to send it off as is to her reader. In reality, though, it probably needs further revision and polishing. A messy handwritten draft, on the other hand, still looks like it needs more work.

This introduction offered some general tips to keep in mind as you begin to compose. Now turn the page to learn how to incorporate specific essential qualities that will increase the effectiveness of your writing.

ONE

Creativity and Originality

Most of us don't write because we enjoy writing or because we have a burning need to pen our thoughts on a topic. Instead, we write mostly to achieve a specific purpose (for example, to apply for a job or to complain about a restaurant's poor service) or to fulfill the reader's need (for example, to give the boss information about a project or to show a history professor that we understand the causes of World War I). Most of the time, then, we don't have to think up topics to write about. Topics are supplied by the situations and people in our lives.

However, even though life "assigns" us topics all the time, we still must strive to present fresh and interesting ideas in everything we write, from business letters to research papers. Thus, all effective writing is creative and original, offering the reader new ideas, new insights, or new perspectives on a topic. Of course, when faced with the task of generating any type of composition, it's easier for the writer simply to rehash old ideas, an approach that requires less research and less thought. But readers read to learn, to increase their knowledge and understanding, so the writer's job is to offer them something they don't already know. If the reader is already familiar with the information in a document, then there's no reason for him to waste his time reading it.

Therefore, when we have some choice in our topic selection (as we often do in academic settings, for instance), we should avoid the same old stale subjects. When a stale subject is unavoidable, we should strive to present a fresh angle or perspective. For example, let's say your subject is the legal drinking age. You need to write an essay for your English class, or maybe you feel compelled to voice your opinions on this topic to your state legislators. You want to argue that the legal drinking age should be eighteen years. This is a stale topic because it's been the subject of many a composition for years. But that doesn't mean you can't write about it, especially if you believe it is an important and worthwhile issue. However, you will want to avoid all of the stale old reasons that many writers before you have presented in defense of this viewpoint. In your composition, like hundreds of others, you will be tempted to offer the following arguments:

1. Eighteen-year-olds are considered legal adults by the U.S. judicial system and military; therefore, they should be considered adults when it comes to drinking.

2. Eighteen-year-olds are just as responsible and mature as twenty-one-year-olds.

3. Eighteen-year-olds drink anyway, so why fight it?

If you offer these reasons in your paper, you'll simply be rehashing the same tired points that everyone has already heard. Instead, you'll need to come up with a new perspective or fresh angle, one the reader has not heard. What are other reasons an eighteen-year-old should be permitted to drink alcohol? For better health? To improve the state's economy? Think of all the possibilities, even those that seem silly or illogical or far-fetched at first. In other words, be creative.

Now, you might be thinking, "Be creative! I can't! I'm not!" That's because you, like most people, probably associate creativity with art, and even though you might play a little piano or dance or draw, you usually don't feel as though you're creating art when you sit down to write. Being creative, however, does not necessarily involve producing art. Instead, being creative involves rejecting existing habits and routines and figuring out new solutions to old problems.[1] A creative person thinks for herself, not limiting herself to the ideas of others. She explores her thoughts, always trying to come up with a better way of doing or understanding something.

In order to be more creative when it comes to the writing you must do in your life, you can do several things all the time, even when you're not faced with a writing project. That way, when you do need to write, you'll have more ideas.

> **Observe the world around you.**   Pay more attention. Look at everything more closely. Notice details. Be curious. Ask questions. Keep up with the news and current events.

> **Be open to more possibilities.**   Don't always accept the prevailing explanations or theories. Question authority. Wonder if there's a better way. Play "What if . . . ?" with yourself or others.

> **Think about it longer.**   Don't simply settle for your first thought. Explore ideas for longer periods of time. Take long walks just to think. Allow yourself some time to daydream.

> **Keep a journal.**   Take it with you everywhere and record random thoughts, ideas, and inspirations as they occur to you, even in the middle of the night.

All of these activities should stimulate your creativity all the time, so you'll be better prepared to be creative in response to a writing task.

Of course, you may object to these suggestions because you doubt there will be any extra rewards in exchange for extra creative effort. You may be thinking, "If I can earn a good grade for a dull research paper on a 'stale' topic, why work so much harder to produce a truly interesting one?" It's true that creative effort does not always pay off with tangible rewards such as more money, promotions, or better grades. However, you can experience some worthwhile *intrinsic* rewards for creativity when you write. You will improve your thinking skills. You will find satisfaction in successfully completing a challenging project. And you may find that the creative process is its own reward; many people experience delight in the act of coming up with something unique.

If you're still not convinced that creativity is worth the trouble, think of noncreative, production-line writing as a waste of your valuable time. If you spent a lot of energy on a hackneyed or uninteresting writing task that did not result in new knowledge or insight for yourself *or* your reader, then the composition did not serve its purpose, and the whole procedure was a waste of effort. Even in your academic writing, strive to give the professor something new. Rather than viewing the writing task as another useless hoop to jump through, view it as an opportunity to share new insights and ideas.

The next sections will offer you specific techniques for stimulating your creativity for your writing projects.

> **TIP:**
>
> *To overcome writer's block, you may need to shut off your "inner critic," the voice inside your head that insists your ideas are worthless or your writing skills are poor. Either ignore this voice or outwit it by pretending that you're only playing around with your ideas, not writing them down "for real."*

The Brain

Before we can understand how to generate fresh, interesting ideas for writing tasks, we need to understand where they come from. Because writing is a mental task, it's helpful to know a little bit about how the brain functions during the composition process.

The brain is divided into two hemispheres that we'll call the right brain and the left brain. Years of research and study have proven that each hemisphere is responsible for different kinds of mental tasks. The left brain is responsible for logical, analytical thinking. It is the organizer, the planner, the part of the brain that thinks in words. The right brain, on the other hand, is responsible for intuitive, emotional thinking. It is the imaginative part of the brain that thinks in pictures.

Left Brain	*Right Brain*
verbal	imagistic
detailed	holistic
sequential	simultaneous
analytical	synthesizing
logical	analogical
informational	conceptual
linear	all at once
convergent	divergent
abstract	concrete
rational	emotional
objective	subjective
intellectual	intuitive

systematic	random
structured	spontaneous

Obviously, *both* sides of the brain must work equally to produce a document. The right brain has to imagine the possibilities and come up with the ideas, and the left brain has to evaluate those ideas and then apply some structure to them so they can be offered to a reader in a coherent package.

However, many of us have a dominant brain hemisphere that is more highly developed and thus controls our mental processes. People with a dominant left brain are often very organized, methodical, serious, and systematic. They prefer routine and habit. They like to plan ahead, make lists, and put things in order. People with a dominant right brain are very often spontaneous, humorous, and artistic. They like to be free to experiment, so they dislike routine.

EXERCISE 1.1   *Left Brain–Right Brain*

To identify your brain dominance, take the following quiz[2]:

1. When meeting someone

    a. I usually show up early or on time.

    b. I am usually running a little late.

2. Daydreaming is

    a. a waste of time.

    b. the best part of my day.

3. When faced with a decision

    a. I weigh all my options and make a decision based on the facts at hand.

    b. I go with my gut (instincts).

4. When learning how to use a new piece of equipment

    a. I read the instruction manual before beginning.

    b. I jump in and wing it. (If all else fails, I'll look at the manual.)

5. When someone gives me directions, I prefer to

    a. have them written out (with street names).

    b. have him draw me a map with landmarks and visual references.

6. When I'm shopping and I see something I want to buy

    a. I save up until I have the money.

    b. I charge it. (You only live once.)

7. When I am telling a story to a friend

    a. I will cut to the chase. (I use the phrase "Yada, yada, yada" a great deal.)

    b. I am very animated and likely to get sidetracked.

8. When I have been faced with major changes in my life, I found it

    a. terrifying.

    b. exciting.

9. Which best describes the cleanliness of where I live:

    a. Martha Stewart would be proud.

    b. Oscar Madison (the messy one) would be proud.

10. When it comes to paper,

    a. I like to file it.

    b. I like to pile it.

11. When it comes to implementing a project, I am likely to be asked to

    a. handle the step-by-step planning and implementation

    b. come up with ideas and deal with the big picture.

12. When it comes to remembering things I have to do,

    a. I remember every little detail.

    b. What was the question again?

13. People describe me as

    a. level-headed (unemotional).

    b. a roller coaster of emotions (passionate).

14. In a nutshell, my work style is like this:

    a. I tend to concentrate on one task at a time; I'm easily overwhelmed.

    b. I like to juggle several things at once.

15. When reading a magazine

    a. I start at page one and read in a sequential order.

    b. I jump in wherever it looks most interesting.

16. When asked for my opinion, I

   a. think before I speak.

   b. say what's on my mind (foot-in-mouth syndrome).

If you have 10 or more "A" answers, you can consider yourself left brain dominant. If you have 10 or more "B" answers, you're a right-brainer.

When it comes to writing, is it better to be more right-brained or left-brained? Neither dominance is better than the other. As a matter of fact, each has its own particular advantages and disadvantages when applied to a writing task. Left-brained writers will, of course, excel at organizing their thoughts into logical patterns. In addition, they will usually be good at breaking the whole composition procedure down into logical, manageable segments and then completing each segment using a step-by-step approach. However, left-brained writers often have difficulty generating ideas. Because their dominant left brain is usually trying to impose structure on every thought that arises, it often inhibits the writer's initial creative efforts. Right-brained writers, on the other hand, have little trouble coming up with lots of unique ideas. They often have so many that they don't know which one to focus on first. But right-brained writers often struggle when it's time to determine an effective order for their thoughts or when they have to explain their ideas with sufficient details.

Such weaknesses, however, can be overcome. Neither the left-brained nor right-brained writer should feel that she'll never master certain aspects of the composition process. Each just needs a repertoire of techniques she can use to capitalize on her strengths and to overcome her weaknesses.

Invention Strategies

"I can't think of anything to write about."

Faced with a writing task, you may have spoken these words at least once. If the project was related to an academic class, you may have struggled to think up a good topic to write about. If the topic was already assigned, perhaps by your boss or your attorney, you may have experienced difficulty thinking up all of the points you needed to make.

Many times when the above words are spoken, the miserable writer utters them after staring in frustration at the wall, the blank paper, or the blank computer screen for minutes or even hours. This technique, which we'll refer to as the "divine inspiration" method of getting ideas, involves sitting in a passive state, waiting for the perfect idea to suddenly be sent from the heavens straight to the brain. It often fails the writer, who gets more and more frustrated and stressed the longer he sits there. The "divine inspiration" method is probably the most common idea-generation technique practiced by inexperienced writers, and it's also the least effective.

Unfortunately, after using this approach, many a beginning writer has concluded that he has no ideas and nothing to say, just because his mind remained as blank as the paper in front of him. Actually, though, *everyone* has important, worthwhile thoughts on a wide variety of topics. Everyone has opinions and ideas, and most people could even be considered experts on at least one subject that interests them. So why do so many people believe they have nothing to write about? Because they rely on a useless technique for finding ideas when the time comes to put their thoughts on paper.

A writer must use a more active approach when she's trying to discover, or invent, something to say. She needs to know and use one or more specific strategies for getting ideas. Such **invention strategies** will help a writer choose a topic, narrow a topic, or decide what she wants to say about a topic.

There is no one best way to go about generating ideas. Different techniques work for different writers. You might prefer brainstorming, for example, while a classmate finds that freewriting works best for him. Certain techniques are also suited for certain kinds of writing tasks. If you need to tell a story, for instance, you might want to use the clustering method, which is a good technique for exploring memories and images. If you need to write an explanation of a new policy for your employees, you might want to use the cubing method, which is a good way to generate specific categorical information. Finally, certain techniques are better suited to overcoming weaknesses stemming from left or right brain dominance. Some methods encourage right brain thinking, so they're particularly effective for the left-brained writer who needs to temporarily bypass her left brain's tendency to evaluate and organize every thought in order to stimulate her right brain to produce more ideas. Other methods result in a more systematic approach to getting ideas, which are more suited to right-brained writers who need to produce a well-organized document.

The invention strategies discussed in the rest of this chapter can be arranged along a right brain–left brain continuum (see page 10). The techniques near the top of the continuum tend to stimulate the right brain, while those near the bottom of the continuum involve the left brain more. You should familiarize yourself with and practice all of these various techniques. Some of them require pencil and paper; others are better suited for those who like the freedom of exploring ideas mentally, without writing anything down. Find the ones that work best for you, but don't limit yourself to just one or two methods. Be willing to try several different techniques for different kinds of writing tasks. Experiment with a combination of techniques to produce the most comprehensive results.

Talking

Talking, which is probably the most underestimated of all the invention strategies, simply involves discussing your ideas informally with someone before beginning to write. It requires no pen or paper, just an interested or supportive person who will listen to you and perhaps ask questions as you explain aloud what you need to write about.

This method relies on the power of language as a tool for helping us understand our thoughts. Many of the topics we have to write about are ones we've never written about or even discussed before. So, even though we may have some ideas or opinions about the subject, as long as they stay solely in our minds, they tend to be fuzzy, shadowy, and half-formed. Only when someone asks us to express those ideas, either orally or in writing, do they crystallize, assume shape and form. Can you remember the last time someone asked you what you thought about a particular topic, perhaps a current event or issue? In the act of searching for the words you needed to communicate your ideas, you probably clarified in your own mind what you knew or believed about that subject. When we must find the right words to express what we're thinking, our thoughts become clearer, and we know better what we think simply by having found the language to share those thoughts with others. As W. H. Auden put it, "How do I know what I think, until I see what I say?"

So talking about your ideas with others prior to composing can be a valuable preliminary step. You will, of course, have to find the right words when you sit down to write, but you will find this challenging mental task to be a lot easier if you've already experimented with it in an informal conversation. Oral discussion will also produce the additional benefit of helping you identify gaps in your information or aspects of the

INVENTION STRATEGIES FOR COMPOSITION

The strategies at the top of the list draw more on your right brain. They are more spontaneous and informal, so they're a good stimulus for creativity. These techniques are all effective ways to generate ideas, particularly for writing that explores the self.

Talking. Explaining verbally to another person what you want to write about.

Drawing. Picturing your subject in images and drawing them.

Brainstorming. Free associating and writing down images and ideas in any order as they occur to you.

Clustering. Recording ideas in the order in which they occur to you as you free associate; exploring different trains of thought.

Meditating. Clearing your mind, then focusing your full attention on your topic and letting ideas and images arise.

Making an analogy. Comparing your subject to something else.

Freewriting. Recording your stream of consciousness in response to a suggested topic.

Cubing. Exploring your topic from different angles: describing it, telling a story about it, analyzing its causes or effects or parts, comparing it, arguing for it, etc.

Listing. Making lists in response to a suggested topic.

Using the journalism method. Like a newspaper reporter, asking the questions: Who? What? When? Where? Why? How?

Answering questions. Creating and answering more specific questions about your subject.

The strategies toward the bottom of the list draw more on your left brain. They are more analytical, structured, and formal. They're good techniques for generating ideas for writing when your goal is to communicate information to an audience.

topic that you're still not sure about. Then you can gather the missing data or spend more time thinking before you begin to write. If you begin writing when you're still fuzzy about what you think, your composition will be fuzzy, too.

The actual writing of any composition is a challenging mental activity. It involves considering the best arrangement of smaller units (your sentences and paragraphs) while keeping the big picture, your overall goal, in mind at the same time. Therefore, writing involves paying attention simultaneously to the microcosm and the macrocosm. It's like flying by helicopter into a forest. As you approach in the air from far away, you can see the whole forest, its overall shape, its edges, its contours. As you fly closer, you lose sight of the boundaries, but then you can distinguish individual trees. As you descend between those trees, you begin to notice their leaves, bark, and other details. When the helicopter deposits you in the middle of the forest, you'll easily lose your way if you can't remember the edges and overall shape of the forest that you saw on your way in. Seeing the details and the big picture all at the same time is a difficult task even for experienced professional writers. So you don't want to add more mental burden to that process by forcing your brain to think up ideas while you compose. Use an invention strategy such as talking to fully understand your thoughts *before* you begin to write.

EXERCISE 1.2   *Talking*

1. With a partner, talk about a current news topic you've never discussed or written about before. Notice how your thinking about this topic becomes clearer as you discuss it.

2. Form a study group with other classmates enrolled in a course you're taking. Notice how oral discussion of the facts and concepts you're learning helps you understand them better.

3. For your next writing task, use the talk strategy to find and clarify ideas before composing.

Drawing

The right side of the brain is responsible for processing visual images. When you picture your subject in your mind, you're using your right hemisphere to generate ideas. Recording those mental pictures by drawing them on paper is a completely right-brained approach to exploring a topic. You don't have to possess artistic talent to use this technique. Forget about producing a creative masterpiece. This method involves sketching your mental images so you can tap into your right brain's capability for remembering pictorial detail.

The drawing technique is especially well suited for writing tasks that ask you to describe a person, place, or object or to explore your memories. For example, your supervisor might ask you to propose a new office layout to improve traffic flow and efficiency. One of your relatives might like more information about the hotel where you stayed in the Bahamas. Or you might need to describe storm damage to your house for an insurance company. Try the drawing invention strategy to help you get ideas before writing.

EXERCISE 1.3   *Drawing*

1. Visualize a place where you spent a lot of time during your childhood. Sketch it on paper.
2. Pretend that you must write a letter nominating a colleague for a "best dressed" or "most stylish" award. Use the drawing technique to help you get ideas.
3. Sketch a beautiful object in your home.
4. Draw a map that illustrates the shortest route from your college's campus to your home.

Brainstorming

Brainstorming involves quickly writing down words and phrases that occur to you as you consider your topic. This technique is based on free association, the concept that one thought leads to another thought. For example, when you hear the word *orange*, another word or picture immediately pops into your mind. When you brainstorm, you record that word or phrase, and then the next one that occurs to you, and then the next. For example, if you began with the word *airplane*, you might generate something like this:

bad food   pilot
landings   wings   expensive
            AIRPLANE   no smoking
take-off crash   fear
              airport   clouds
trip to Florida   stewardesses   747

To most effectively use the brainstorming technique, follow these guidelines:

Don't try to organize your thoughts in any way. Let your right brain do the work. Don't try to impose any order on your thoughts. Just let them arise randomly. Don't record them in any certain order, either, even if your paper gets messy. Fill up a sheet of paper by writing down each word or phrase anywhere on the blank page, as the example above illustrates.

Don't censor any of your ideas. Write down every word or phrase that pops into your mind, even if one seems silly or irrelevant. Take dictation of your thoughts. You can weed out the useless or unrelated ideas later. During brainstorming, don't evaluate or judge, just record.

Do write as fast as you can and continue to record ideas until they stop coming to you.

Brainstorming is an effective, informal way to explore your thoughts. It's also a good technique for narrowing ideas. For example, if your history professor assigns a term paper on the Vietnam War, you might brainstorm on the topic to help you zero in on some specific aspect to focus on. Then you could brainstorm again on your new limited topic, such as one specific battle or one particular military commander.

Furthermore, brainstorming is a great technique for problem solving. If, for instance, your supervisor wants you to come up with some ideas for advertising or marketing your company's product or service, you could write *possible new marketing strategies* on a sheet of paper and then allow your right brain to fill up the page with possibilities, even seemingly impractical or extravagant ideas (they might turn out to be innovative later). If you need to solve a personal problem, such as trying to get your family members to help you with the housework, get out some paper and brainstorm a variety of possible solutions.

EXERCISE 1.4 *Brainstorming*

1. Choose your favorite holiday (Thanksgiving, Fourth of July, your birthday, etc.) and brainstorm your ideas about and images of that celebration.

2. What inventions does the world need? Brainstorm on this topic.

3. Pretend your biology instructor has assigned you to write about a recent medical breakthrough. Use the brainstorming technique to limit the topic, then brainstorm a second time to generate ideas about the one specific breakthrough you chose.

4. Think of a personal problem you need to solve. Brainstorm some possible solutions.

TIP:

It's better to explain a smaller, more specific topic in detail than merely to skim the surface of a larger, broader topic.

Clustering

Like brainstorming, clustering is based on free association, the mind's tendency to link one thought to another. But clustering assumes that ideas don't pop into our heads in an isolated, random fashion, but in trains of thought or "clusters." A cluster, then, is a collection of related ideas. This method is slightly more organized than brainstorming because you link ideas together in a chain in the order in which they occur to you, exhausting one set of associations before beginning another set. For example, you begin, as in brainstorming, with a topic. You write down the first word or phrase you think of when you consider that topic. Then you write down what that word or phrase makes you think of, and so on. So, for example, if you began with the word *beach*, your clustering might look something like this:

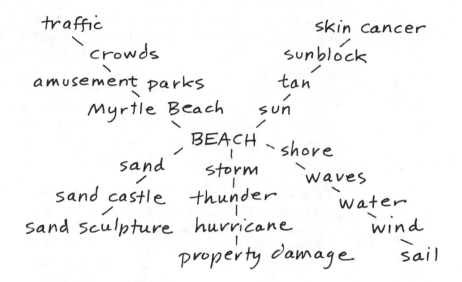

You follow a train of thought as far as you can, then return to your original topic to begin another train of thought. When you finish, you'll have several sets of associations, or clusters. Like brainstorming, this technique is most effective when you don't censor yourself, instead writing everything quickly to capture every idea and image. Clustering is a useful method for narrowing a topic to a more specific focus.

EXERCISE 1.5   *Clustering*

1. Create a cluster of ideas for one of the following words: *summer, pet, grandmother, college.*

2. Think of an idea or a concept you recently studied in one of your classes. Cluster it.

Meditating

Another useful technique for generating ideas is meditation, which involves clearing your mind, focusing your full attention on your topic, and letting ideas and images arise. Meditation does not necessarily require sitting cross-legged in an incense-filled room and chanting, our stereotyped image of this activity. Rather, it requires focused concentration that can be accomplished in a variety of positions and settings.

If you've tried any form of meditation, you know it can be very difficult to accomplish the first step of clearing the mind. Our brains are always filled with a lot of different thoughts competing for our attention. Things to do, plans to make, problems to solve—all jostle each other constantly, each demanding our consideration. Temporarily banishing all of this mental noise to a dark corner of your mind while you concentrate on one specific project, such as an essay you need to write for your English class, can be challenging. But you can use some specific techniques for sweeping away the clutter for a while so you can focus on just one idea:

> **Before you attempt to focus on one particular idea or project, spend a little time devoting your full attention to all of the other thoughts that might intrude.** Either mentally or on paper, take ten minutes to concentrate exclusively on your boyfriend, your problem at work, your upcoming math test, or anything else that will pull your attention away from your writing. If you can't stop thinking about all of the other things you need to be doing, take five or ten minutes to make a "to do" list. Then you might find it easier to focus solely on your ideas for your composition.

> **Try mental visualization techniques to clear your mind.** This method is similar to the "counting sheep" procedure some people use to go to sleep. When you mentally visualize sheep jumping a fence one after the other, you're attempting to distract your mind from all of the buzzing thoughts that keep you from relaxing. Other visualization techniques involve envisioning certain images or scenarios in order to quiet your mind. One method, for example, tells you to picture a platform or stage. Then visualize yourself standing on the platform holding a broom. Every time a thought surfaces in your consciousness, picture it as a little gremlin trying to crawl up onto your platform, and see yourself sweeping it back

into the shadows with your broom. Sweep off all thoughts that try to get up onto the clear, smooth platform of your mind until they stop trying. Then focus your full attention of your composition topic. Another method involves visualizing yourself in deep, clear water. Imagine going beneath the surface and still being able to breathe. You will sink lower and lower, to deeper, more silent levels as you proceed, but you first envision yourself spending some time just below the surface. Picture your thoughts as aquatic creatures swimming by. Let them drift and swim around you for a while, noticing and watching each one, then imagine yourself descending deeper, to another level. At each level, the numbers of thought "creatures" will diminish until you feel you're in a still, quiet place too deep for any of them.[3] Then think about your composition topic. If you'd like to know more about other such visualization methods, the many books about meditation can offer other techniques for clearing the mind of its clutter.

Take advantage of "mental down time." We engage in a lot of activities each day that don't require much thought. These activities—such as doing the dishes, taking a shower, jogging, or even driving a car—are ones we do without having to think about what we're doing, as though we're on autopilot. As a result, they afford good opportunities for mini-meditation sessions about ideas. While engaged in these activities, try focusing your attention on a topic you need to write about. When you're finished, you might want to jot down what you came up with for further consideration later.

 EXERCISE 1.6   *Meditating*

Try one or more of the techniques discussed in this section to see if any of them works for you.

TIP:

Try meditation techniques to clear your mind of clutter before composing. Then you'll be free to concentrate on writing.

Making an Analogy

An analogy is a creative comparison between two unlike things that reveals interesting, thought-provoking points about a topic. Analogies also help us understand a new idea by relating it to something we're already familiar with. Earlier in this chapter, for example, the comparison of writing to flying by helicopter into a forest should have helped you better understand the nature of the composition process. Here are a few more analogies:

Life is like a jigsaw puzzle, but you don't have the picture on the front of the box to know what it's supposed to look like. Sometimes, you're not even sure if you have all the pieces.[4]

Planet Earth is 4,600 million years old. If we condense this inconceivable time span into an understandable concept, we can liken Earth to a person of 46 years of age. Nothing is known about the first 7 years of this person's life, and whilst only scattered information exists about the middle span, we know that only at age 42 did the Earth begin to flower. Dinosaurs and great reptiles did not appear until one year ago, when the planet was 45. Mammals arrived only 8 months ago; in the middle of last week man-like apes evolved into ape-like men, and on the weekend the last ice age enveloped the Earth. Modern man has been around for four hours. During the last hour, Man discovered agriculture. The industrial revolution began a minute ago.[5]

An analogy [for understanding writing procrastination] might be made with diets. There are over two hundred diet books currently on the market, and innumerable spas and clinics are available to help people shed weight. Yet, according to an article in the *Washington Post,* out of every two hundred people who go on a diet, only one loses the weight and keeps it off. The reason, as many psychologists are starting dramatically to realize, is that diets treat the symptom of fat and never address the more fundamental problem of why people overeat in the first place. Any device—a new pencil, fresh paper, a clean desk—that primes the writing pump will temporarily treat the symptoms of writer's block, just as eating celery sticks instead of hot fudge sundaes will take the pounds off for a week.[6]

Comparing your topic to something else can be an effective way to understand it better or to generate ideas.

EXERCISE 1.7   *Making an Analogy*

Complete the following analogies:

1. The first day of college is like _____.

2. Learning something new is like _____.

3. Dieting is like _____.

4. Going on a blind date is like _____.

Freewriting

Freewriting involves recording your stream of consciousness, the flow of thought in your mind. When you freewrite, you literally take dictation from your brain, letting your thoughts arise freely without controlling them in any way. You can begin with a particular topic to focus on, or just record the mental "noise" going on in your head. This technique is situated near the middle of the right brain–left brain continuum, so it's an excellent tool for generating ideas for a wide variety of writing tasks. It will also help you understand what you already know about your topic.

In order to freewrite most effectively, follow these guidelines:

Write for a prescribed length of time, say ten or fifteen minutes. During that time, do not stop writing. If your mind goes blank, write "my mind is blank my mind is blank" over and over until another thought occurs to you.

Don't censor your thoughts.   Write down everything you're thinking, even if it seems silly or irrelevant. Don't judge or evaluate your thoughts now—just get them down onto the page. If your train of thought moves away from your original topic to another subject, let it.

Forget about grammar and spelling.   Don't worry about punctuation, capital letters, or the spelling of words. When you freewrite, your right brain will be more productive if you abandon all of the rules. Don't slow yourself down by wondering whether you should use a comma or a semicolon. Write as fast as you can, and don't try to write complete sentences. The brain thinks in fragments and phrases, so your freewriting should be a collection of partial and half-formed thoughts. As a result, you'll probably end up with sloppy, seemingly incomprehensible scribblings. If someone else were to read your freewriting, it probably wouldn't make any sense to him. But it's not meant for others to read. No one but you will see these pages—this activity is a tool for the writer as you explore your ideas. Later on, you'll sculpt them into a document suitable for the reader's eyes.

Beyond generating ideas, freewriting can be helpful in other ways. Like brainstorming, it can be an effective tool for problem solving and self-understanding. When something is bothering you, spend some time emptying your thoughts onto paper. This is a good technique for both identifying the source of the problem and then generating some possible solutions. Also, freewriting is an effective tool for clearing your mind of its clutter before you begin a task, like writing a memo, that will demand your full concentration. Freewrite to give your other thoughts some attention. Then they'll be less likely to intrude when you need to focus your mental efforts on one particular project.

TIP:

For another good problem-solving tool, review the section on brainstorming beginning on page 12.

EXERCISE 1.8   *Freewriting*

1. Freewrite for ten minutes on one of the following topics:

   A Challenge I Face

   My Goals

   Things About Myself I'd Like to Improve

2. Choose one particular topic from your field of study that you're interested in knowing more about. Freewrite on this topic for ten minutes to discover what you already know about it.

3. Freewrite without beginning with a specific topic. Simply record the mental noise going on inside your head at this moment.

Cubing

The rest of the invention strategies on the continuum, beginning with cubing, take a more formal, more structured approach to discovering ideas. Rather than letting ideas arise spontaneously from the right brain, these methods ask the writer to think in more specific ways, drawing on the left brain's ability to produce ideas in a more systematic manner.

In cubing, you begin with a particular topic and then explore the different aspects of that topic, as though you were examining the different faces of a cube. You describe it, tell a story about it, compare or contrast it to something else, tell how to do it, give examples of it, analyze its causes or effects, divide it, classify it, define it, or argue for it. "It" can be either the original topic itself or some narrowed aspect of that topic. Try to come up with several ideas in each category. For example, if your topic is golf, your cubing might look like this:

Describe it

- distinguishing features of golf
- a specific golf course
- regulation golf attire

Tell a story about it

- my first attempt to play
- my trip to the Master's tournament
- my best golf game

Compare or contrast it

- 1800's golf versus golf today
- spike shoes versus soft-sole shoes
- one top golfer versus another

Tell how to do it

- perfecting your swing
- improving your putting

Give examples of it

- the best golf resorts
- top professional golfers

Analyze its causes or effects

- reasons for its growing popularity
- benefits of learning to play

Divide it

- components of a golf course

Classify it

- types of golfers
- types of courses

Define it

- what is golf?

Argue for it

- why you should learn to play
- why a specific brand of clubs is superior

For a comprehensive report on the topic, you may need to include a lot of the information and ideas in the lists above. Or you might—depending on your purpose and reader—select one specific focus. Do you want to persuade the salespeople you supervise to take up the game? Then you'll focus on the ideas in your "argue for it" category. Do you want to explain to your brother why you love the game? Select ideas from the "describe it" or "analyze its effects" categories. Do you need to write a report for your physical education instructor? You may want to explain what you learned about how to play golf. Cubing is a very orderly way to discover a lot of ideas about one topic or to narrow a topic.

EXERCISE 1.9 **Cubing**

Try cubing at least one of the following topics:

Your field of study (nursing, engineering, education, etc.)

One of your hobbies or interests

The college you attend

TIP:

Try to write in an environment free of distractions such as the television, radio, ringing phone, and other people. You'll be able to concentrate better if you can work uninterrupted.

Listing

Listing is another orderly way to generate ideas. It's like brainstorming because you write down words or phrases related to your topic. However, it's more structured in two ways. First, you usually set a target number of items to produce (for example, ten ways to save money on household utilities, or five reasons for joining a campus club). Second, rather than writing the items randomly across the page, as you do when you brainstorm, you impose more order by lining them up in a column and numbering them. You might also arrange your list using certain patterns, such as most important to least important or lowest to highest.

You can also use this technique to generate the main points you'd like to make about your subject. For example, if your topic is teacher competency tests, you could list all of the ideas you'd like to include in your composition:

1. Unfair to teachers
2. No equivalent test in other professions
3. College degree should be enough proof of competency
4. Teachers already take certification exams
5. Competency tests don't solve the real problem

Left-brained people, who tend to be fond of making lists, use them to remember things and to set priorities. Lists can also be valuable tools for discovering ideas, arranging them, and pushing yourself to think more about the topic than you would otherwise. If you numbered your paper to ten and you have written only seven items, chances are that you'll continue to ponder the subject in hopes of completing the list.

EXERCISE 1.10   *Listing*

Create the following lists:

Six Things I'd Like to Change

Five Ways to Generate More Business at My Place of Employment

Eight Habits of Successful Students

Three Best Restaurants in This Town

Using the Journalism Method

When a reporter goes out to collect information about an event or situation, she gets answers to the following questions: Who? What? When? Where? Why? How? Asking (and finding answers to) these questions about your topic can be an effective way to generate ideas. For example, if you've been assigned to evaluate a particular software package for your office, you could explore different aspects by asking questions such as:

Who designed this software?

Who manufactures it?

> *What* can the software do?
>
> *What* are its distinguishing features?
>
> *When* did it first become available?
>
> *When* was it last updated?
>
> *When* can you expect it to arrive after placing an order?
>
> *Where* should it be installed? (Does everyone in the office need it?)
>
> *Why* is this company's product better than other products?
>
> *Why* do we need it in our office?
>
> *How* much does it cost?
>
> *How* will the manufacturer help us install and maintain it?
>
> *How* will we pay for it?

Investigating the answers to all of these questions should provide you with a lot of good ideas for the report or memo you need to write.

EXERCISE 1.11 ## Using the Journalism Method

Generate specific who, what, when, where, why, and how questions for at least one of the following topics. Then jot down answers to each question.

A specific disease affecting yourself, a relative, or a friend

A place you'd like to visit

An area or procedure at work that is unsafe or inefficient

A campus club you belong to

Answering Questions

You might view this final invention strategy as a combination of cubing and the journalism approach. As in the journalism method, you answer who, what, when, where, why, and how questions about your topic. But these questions are more specific, related to particular aspects or facets of the subject. Here is one possible list of such questions:

1. How can *X* be described?
2. How did *X* happen?

3. What kind of person is X?

4. What is my memory of X?

5. What is my personal response to X?

6. What are the facts about X?

7. How can X be summarized?

8. What does X mean?

9. What is the essential function of X?

10. What are the component parts of X?

11. How is X made or done?

12. How should X be made or done?

13. What are the causes of X?

14. What are the consequences of X?

15. What are the types of X?

16. How does X compare to Y?

17. What is the present status of X?

18. How should X be interpreted?

19. What is the value of X?

20. What case can be made for or against X?[7]

As in cubing, your goal is to produce a variety of specific questions so that you can explore many different angles of your main topic. For example, if your art professor asks you to write about some aspect of modern art, substitute the phrase *modern art* (or the name of a specific modern artist) for the X in each of the above questions. Then, by considering the answers to the resulting questions, you should generate a lot of different potential topics for your composition.

EXERCISE 1.12   *Answering Questions*

Use the list of twenty questions above to generate more specific questions related to one of the following topics:

Recycling

Poetry

Labor Unions

Low-fat Cooking

Internal Revenue Service

The Internet

Cigarettes

Then choose five of the specific questions you generated and jot down ideas in response to each one.

All of the strategies discussed in this chapter unlock the many ideas in your head in various ways. If one method fails you, try another. Mix the methods, perhaps a right-brained technique with a left-brained technique, to generate a wider range of ideas. With so many varied invention strategies at your disposal, you need never again stare at a blank sheet of paper in despair and frustration. When you know how to use all of these methods and have discovered which ones work best for you, you'll never again lament that you "can't think of anything to write about." Furthermore, your thoughts—and the documents that express them—will be more clever, more original, and more creative.

Chapter Summary

We use both the right and left hemispheres of the brain to generate ideas for writing. **Invention strategies** are the different techniques we can use to discover what we need to say. Some of these strategies draw on the right brain's ability to think in holistic pictures, while others are produced more systematically by the structured left brain. We writers can **talk** informally to our friends about what we want to write or **draw** pictures to stimulate our visual memories of a topic. We can **brainstorm** or **cluster** ideas, quickly recording the free associations that arise in our minds. We can **meditate,** clearing our minds of clutter so we can focus our full attention on the topic. We can create **analogies,** which are clever comparisons. We can **freewrite,** recording our stream of consciousness. We can explore different aspects of a topic through **cubing,** or jot down ideas in **list** form. Or we can generate and **answer questions** or use the **journalism method.**

A writer can experiment with combinations of these invention techniques to find the most original, creative ideas for his compositions.

Suggested Writing Activities

Use at least one invention strategy to discover ideas for the following compositions:

1. Describe a place where you spent a lot of time during your childhood.

2. Write a letter nominating a colleague for a "best dressed" or "most stylish" award.

3. Write an essay to argue that a particular object in your home is beautiful.

4. Write about your favorite holiday.

5. Write a report about a recent medical breakthrough.

6. Write a report about an idea or concept you recently studied in one of your classes.

7. Write about your first day of college.

8. Write a report about your field of study.

9. Write a memo to your supervisor proposing ways to generate more business at your place of employment.

10. Tell a story about a time you were in danger.

Notes

1. S. I. Hayakawa, *Through the Communication Barrier* (New York: Harper & Row, 1979), 104.

2. Lee Silber, *Time Management for the Creative Person* (New York: Crown, 1998), 7–11. Copyright © 1998 by Lee Silber. Reprinted by permissionof the Crown Publishing Group.

3. Wayne Dyer, *Your Sacred Self* (New York: HarperCollins, 1995), 147–152.

4. Roger von Oech, *A Whack on the Side of the Head* (New York: Warner Books, 1990), 51.

5. Tom McArthur, ed., *The Oxford Companion to the English Language* (Oxford: Oxford University Press, 1992), 63.

6. Henriette Anne Klauser, *Writing on Both Sides of the Brain* (San Francisco: HarperSanFrancisco, 1987), 58.

7. Jacqueline Berke, *Twenty Questions for the Writer* (San Diego: Harcourt Brace Jovanovich, 1985), ix–x.

TWO

Vivid Language

*M*ost of us would agree that this passage from a magazine is an example of good writing:

Humpback Bridge sits like a wooden rainbow over the broad waters of Dunlap Creek, near Covington, Virginia. Gray-brown, wooden corduroy sides bathe in the glow of the setting sun and melt in a golden pool against the Allegheny Mountains. A sudden breeze grabs a swirling mass of glittering yellow leaves off their branches, scattering some on the green, grassy slope and some into the creek. The earth trembles, and the hypnotic quiet is interrupted as a train lumbers across the trestle that sits near this grand old bridge, constructed in 1835.[1]

Why is this good writing? You might answer that it's good because it's very detailed or because it paints a picture in your mind. Writing that creates mental pictures is writing that is communicating with the reader. We create these pictures by using vivid language, words that help the reader form mental images that help him understand the writer's meaning. The brief passage above is effective because it contains all four aspects of vivid language: (1) factual and sensory details, (2) strong verbs, (3) descriptive adjectives, and (4) figures of speech. In this excerpt, the writer is trying to create for the reader a mental image of a covered bridge. He does this by including factual details (the specific names of the bridge, the creek, the town, and the mountains, as well as the bridge's date of construction), sensory details (the colors of the bridge, the leaves, and the slope, as well as the sounds of the quiet and the train), strong verbs (*sits, bathe, melt, grabs, trembles, lumbers*), descriptive adjectives (*wooden, broad, corduroy, sudden, swirling, glittering, grassy, hypnotic, grand, old*), and figures of speech such as simile (*sits like a wooden rainbow*) and personification (*sides bathe in the glow*). These are the types of language that bring your ideas alive.

Details

Meanings are in people, not in words. Words are arbitrary combinations of letters and sounds that we decide will designate certain things or ideas. Words can suggest different meanings to different people, so it's important when you write to choose the language that leaves no doubt about what exactly you, the writer, mean. When you use specific, detailed language, you will not risk that the reader, who may attach to your words a different meaning than you intended, will misunderstand you.

General Versus Specific Language

Words have different levels of generality. For example, examine the following list:

> transportation
>
> vehicle
>
> car
>
> sports car
>
> Corvette
>
> white 1979 Corvette
>
> white 1979 Corvette with a cracked windshield

The items in this list move from very general (transportation, a category that includes a lot of different modes of travel, including boats and airplanes) to very specific (one particular car). The more general the word, the greater the risk of miscommunication with the reader. For example, when you use a word such as *vehicle,* the reader will, at best, conjure up in his mind a shadowy image of something with four tires and, at worst, attach a meaning (truck or motorcycle, for instance) that you did not intend at all. The more specific you can be, the sharper and clearer the image you generate in the reader's mind, and the less likely it is that the reader will misinterpret you.

Bad writing is often filled with general language, words that are too vague or too broad to create a specific mental picture for the reader. If you're writing a memo to a co-worker asking her to send flowers to a client, she might send a bunch of carnations when you meant her to send roses. If you're writing a letter to your local newspaper editor, readers will misunderstand your point if you fail to clarify that you're protesting not taxes for everyone, but property taxes for retirees. In both instances, the writing is bad because it did not fulfill its purpose. It did not fulfill its purpose because one or two general words allowed the readers to decide on meanings the writer did not intend.

As you compose, evaluate each word choice to determine whether you're choosing a general word when a more specific one is more appropriate. Don't write the word *dog* when you really mean *rottweiler.* Don't choose the word *machine* when you really mean *typewriter.* Don't write *beverage* when you mean *sweetened iced tea.* In the following examples, note how the meaning becomes clearer when the general language (in *italics*) is revised to be more specific:

GENERAL: I relaxed by lying under a *tree* listening to *music.*

MORE SPECIFIC: I relaxed by lying under a shady oak listening to an Aerosmith CD.

GENERAL: The *man's operation* was a success.

MORE SPECIFIC: Fred Davis's appendectomy was a success.

GENERAL: *Menial labor jobs* await those without a high school diploma.

MORE SPECIFIC: Frying hamburgers, sweeping floors, and working on assembly lines are common jobs awaiting those without a high school diploma.

GENERAL: Prosthetics have advanced beyond mere *substitutions to the ability to restore function.*

MORE SPECIFIC: Prosthetics have advanced beyond wooden legs and glass eyes to new devices, such as cochlear implants for the ears, which restore the patient's use of the missing or defective body part.

As a final example, read these two versions of the same passage from a newsletter. The first relies heavily on general language. The second substitutes more specific words that make the meaning clearer.

Too many *institutions* depend on *individuals with disabilities* to alert them to problems with their *compliance system* as their primary form of *monitoring.* All *compliance procedures* should include *monitoring provisions* that require a regular *assessment* of the effectiveness of the system and ensure that *modifications* are made when they are warranted. Further, direct and quick *action* should be taken to address *violations* of institutional *policies and procedures.* This must include holding *individuals* accountable who improperly deny *accommodations* to *individuals with disabilities* and/or are guilty of *discriminatory behavior.*[2]

This passage is difficult to comprehend even after two or three readings. The substitution of more specific language makes the meaning much clearer:

Too many colleges depend primarily on disabled students themselves to alert them when college faculty and staff fail to comply with the Americans with Disabilities Act. Instead, colleges should monitor their employees with a system that would help them identify violations of the law and make changes when necessary. Further, these violations of ADA regulations should be quickly identified and corrected. This must include disciplining any college employee who denies legally mandated assistance, such as extra time to take tests, to any disabled student.

Factual and Sensory Details

Clear and interesting writing includes not only specific word choices, but also factual and sensory details. Factual details include information such as names, quantities, dates, and dimensions. For instance, in the list on page 30, the reader's mental image is sharpened with information such as "Corvette" (the type of car) and "1979" (the year of the car). Describing a person as eighty years old and five feet five inches tall provides factual details that help the reader form a clearer picture of the subject. In the following passage from a student's essay on the effects of clear-cutting, the writer has not included many factual details. The italicized questions indicate opportunities for more specific information:

South American rain forests are vanishing [how fast?]. Plants in rain forests [which ones?] supply a large percentage [how much?] of the earth's oxygen. As the trees are cut down [by whom?], plants [like what?] used in medical cures [like what?] are being destroyed [by whom?]. Also, animals [which ones?] are left homeless when their habitat disappears.

Adding the facts would bring the subject into crisper, clearer focus:

South American rain forests are vanishing at the rate of fifty million acres per year. Because the trees, shrubs, vines, and other plants in rain forests supply the earth with much of our planet's oxygen, the rapid depletion of these forests is alarming. As timber companies cut down trees, they also destroy plants, such as the rosy periwinkle, that are becoming important to medical researchers searching for cures for cancer and other diseases. Also, the destruction of rain forests hastens the extinction of birds, insects, reptiles, and other animals, which are left homeless when their habitat vanishes.

Sensory details sharpen the reader's mental image by providing sight, smell, taste, touch, or sound information. For example, that five-foot, five-inch eighty-year-old you're describing may have wispy gray hair (a sight detail), a raspy, cough-racked voice (a sound detail), and dry, papery skin (a touch detail). Each detail you add makes the subject come more alive on the page.

In the following example from a student's narrative essay about a motorcycle race, adding a few sensory details can bring the experience to life on the page.

First version:
I sat on the starting line, ready to go. I wasn't as nervous as I'd been earlier that day, but I still had a few butterflies in my stomach. A man held up a sign with a big number two, which meant two minutes until the gate dropped. All of the racers revved their motors and watched the sign. The man flipped it suddenly to reveal a number one: one minute to go. I was instantly nervous again.

This writer includes some effective sight details but could add more information from his other senses, such as sound, smell, and touch, to help recreate his experience.

Revised to add sensory detail:
I sat on the starting line, ready to go. The buzz of twenty idling motorcycle engines roared in my ears. My bike vibrated beneath me, anxious to spring to life. The sharp smell of gasoline filled my head. I wasn't as nervous as I'd been earlier that day, but I still had a few butterflies in my stomach. The race official held up a sign with a big number two, which meant two minutes until the starting gate dropped. All of the other racers revved their motors, drowning out the cheers of the crowd, and watched the sign. The official flipped it suddenly to reveal a number one: one minute to go. I was instantly nervous again. My hands felt slippery inside my gloves, and my heart pounded.

In this next passage from a student's essay on the benefits of walking, the writer has included few sensory details:

Walking improves your appearance. It helps firm, shape, and tone your body. Walking also improves posture.

Now note how adding sensory information, in addition to a few factual details, helps the reader visualize the subject for improved understanding:

Walking improves your appearance by firming and shaping your body. You will lose excess flab from your legs and buttocks so your thighs won't rub together anymore. Your calf muscles will become more taut and defined. Your buttock muscles will tighten and no longer sag. You'll lose the fat around your torso, resulting in a more slender waistline. Finally, your posture will improve as your spine straightens from regular exercise, allowing you to breathe more efficiently.

Specific language and details will bring your ideas to life and make them easier to grasp.

EXERCISE 2.1   *Details*

Specific Language

Rewrite these sentences to replace the italicized general words or phrases with more specific choices.

1. By beginning a plantwide program that places marked *containers* in *strategic locations* to collect *recyclable material,* this company could recycle one third of *what it sends off to landfill.*

2. Over the past five years, *government funding* for the *elderly* has been significantly *reduced.*

3. The playground will include *playground equipment* along with an open area for the children to play *different games.*

4. Failing to achieve *high goals* in tough *competition* today can result in *withdrawal* and *indifference.*

5. Instead of raising the legal drinking age, *they* should just *get tougher* on *drunk driving.*

6. The kitchen staff shall exhibit personal cleanliness and *conform to hygienic practices.*

7. Long-range planning can help you enjoy your retirement years. The *choices* you make now will determine your standard of living during retirement. *Proper preparation* will ensure that you'll live the life you dream of, with *vacations, material comforts,* and plenty of money for your hobbies and interests.

Factual Details

Insert facts that answer the questions in brackets in the following paragraph:

During high school [name of school? what grade?], I thought I could handle work and make good grades at the same time. So I got a job [where? doing what?] working during the week [when?] and on weekends [when?], sometimes until late at night [how late?]. As a result, I never completed my assignments [for what classes?], and I never got enough sleep [how much did you get?]. So my grades dropped [how much?].

Sensory Details

Rewrite the following paragraph, adding sense information:

Clear-cut timberland is very unattractive. It creates a wasteland. Clear-cutting also decreases property values of nearby homes.

> **TIP:**
>
> *Try to write during the time of day when you're most alert. If you're at your mental peak in the morning, write in the morning. If you're a night owl, write at night.*

Descriptive Adjectives

The second type of vivid language is descriptive adjectives. Adjectives are words that describe nouns. They tell how many, what kind, or which one. The italicized words below are all descriptive adjectives:

the *blue* socks

a *friendly* salesperson

two friends

those carrots

the boy *wearing the hat*

the dress *that she borrowed*

This kind of descriptive information, combined with specific details, helps create clear images in your reader's mind. Adjectives are especially important when we describe something, such as an object, a person, or a place. They provide the important information the reader must have if he is to "see" what you saw. For example, notice how the writer of the following paragraph uses describing words to help you picture the subject:

My *mother's* hands are *beautiful.* They soothed *tiny* cuts on my *baby* knee, stroked my hair when they could not touch my *broken* heart, and remembered not to pat my cheeks after I visited the *oral* surgeon. With her *amazing* hands, my mother can quiet *screaming* children, make *wonderful* food, and braid my *unruly* hair. Her hands trail along walls when she walks and roam over countertops in search of the lid *she's just set down.* My mother used to tell me that since her eyes didn't work very well, God had put *lots of tiny* eyes on her fingers.[3]

The next passage is from an advertisement for a house plan. The first example, which includes few adjectives, offers a flat, lifeless description of the subject:

A porch receives guests entering the house through a foyer—rare amenities for a home. The foyer opens into a room with a fireplace. In the dining room, windows create a setting for meals. The kitchen is designed in a layout with access to other rooms.

A few spicy adjectives create a clearer and more persuasive version to entice the prospective homeowner:

A *wide, shady front* porch receives guests entering the house through a *separate, raised* foyer—*rare* amenities for a *newly built* home *of any size.* The foyer opens into a *spacious living* room with a *welcoming* fireplace. In the *adjacent dining* room, *five* windows *spanning two walls* create a *cheerful, sun-splashed* setting for meals. The kitchen is designed in a *modified galley* layout with *easy* access to the *dining* room, the *center* hall, and the *combination utility–laundry* room.[4]

Adjectives are important not only for describing things, but also for clarifying your ideas. In the following passage from a letter, the writer has included no adjectives:

Does a diploma guarantee you success? That depends. The need for employees is increasing, but many jobs require skilled workers. Earning a diploma usually gives you the training necessary for success.

The reader finds it difficult to understand the subject and the writer's point about that subject. But add a few adjectives, and note how the writer's meaning becomes clearer:

Does a *college* diploma guarantee you *long-term career* success? That depends. The need for *entry-level* employees *in many fields* is increasing, but many of these jobs require *trained* and *educated* people with *effective communication* skills. Earning a *college* diploma usually gives you training in *crucial reading, writing, and speaking* skills that contribute to *professional* success.

However, beware of overusing adjectives. You do not want to pile too many of them in front of your nouns, for too many can slow the pace of your sentences and bog down your ideas with a lot of unnecessary information. In the examples below, many of the adjectives are merely adding extra words without any additional meaning:

TOO MANY ADJECTIVES:	She could see the vampire's glistening, white, sharp fangs gleaming. [*Glistening* and *gleaming* mean the same thing. *Sharp* is an unnecessary modifier for *fangs.*]
REVISION:	She could see the vampire's white fangs gleaming.
TOO MANY ADJECTIVES:	A small, thin, rolled piece of paper filled with tobacco can seize control of your life.
REVISION:	A roll of tobacco-filled paper can seize control of your life.
TOO MANY ADJECTIVES:	Most Americans exhibit negative, unsympathetic, rejecting feelings for mentally ill people.
REVISION:	Many unsympathetic Americans reject mentally ill people.

If you're placing two or three modifiers in front of every person, place, or thing you mention, go back and carefully evaluate each of your describing words. Select only those that seem essential. If you have a tendency to use too many modifiers, you might also be using adjectives to convey meaning that is more effectively delivered by your verbs, the topic of the next section.

EXERCISE 2.2   ## Adjectives

Fill in the first blank with a descriptive adjective (some suggestions: *busy, sad, beautiful, nostalgic*). Then rewrite the rest of the paragraph, adding adjectives to modify each noun in italics.

Fall is a _____ season. *Leaves* drift from the *trees.* The *nights* lengthen, and the *air* cools. *Children* return to *school. Squirrels* store *food* for *winter,* and *birds* ready themselves for their *flight* south. *Snow* is not far away.

TIP:

> *Don't try to revise your sentences as you write them for the first time. Instead, write your entire draft quickly, keeping your overall goal and purpose in mind. Later, you can tinker with the wording of individual sentences.*

Strong Verbs

Clear, interesting writing always relies on strong action verbs to express ideas. A verb is the part of speech in a sentence that conveys the subject's action or state of being. The more descriptive the verb, the sharper the image in the reader's mind. Read the following passage from a magazine article about music, and notice how the verbs add action and life to even an abstract subject:

Not all forms of music *are faring* equally well, however. Western classical music, notably, has had a hard time maintaining its balance in this kaleidoscopic culture. For centuries, it *comprised* the entire superculture: it had no name; it was Music. Folk songs, dances, and religious music *disappeared* into its fabric. At some point during the lifetime of Richard Wagner, classical music *overstepped* the mark and *turned* megalomaniacal. Precisely because it *advertised* itself as universal, superior, and difficult, it *stumbled* badly in the new democratic marketplace. Jazz became the dominant form in the nineteen-thirties and forties; rather quicker on its feet, it *made* a vibrant alliance with Tin Pan Alley while acquiring intellectual cachet by way of bebop. Then all genres *had to bow* before rock and roll, with its promise of global sexual and political liberation. But this revolution soon *split* apart as the more creative elements of punk and alternative rock *renounced* commercial values. Now nothing *holds* the center, and subcultures *run* amok.[5]

This next example is from a newspaper report about the activity of a state legislature:

The House *approved* a bill giving counties the authority to use zoning power to regulate intensive hog operations. The bill, approved 95–23, *imposes* a one-year moratorium on new or expanding hog operations, *increases* the required distances between hog farms and outdoor recreation areas, and *requires* public notice before a hog operation is developed.[6]

Boring writing is filled with boring verbs. As you write, you may have a tendency to choose the first lackluster verbs that occur to you. You might be relying on weak *to be* or *to have* verbs. Though these verbs have their uses, and you cannot write without them, you might be choosing them instead of a more interesting alternative. In the following examples, the dull verbs are italicized. Note how each revision substitutes a much more action-oriented choice:

WEAK VERBS: It *was* in Colorado Springs that we *went* up the highest mountain in the western United States.

STRONG VERB: In Colorado Springs, we *climbed* the highest mountain in the western United States.

WEAK VERB: The whole pan of lasagna fell off the table and *went* all over the floor.

STRONG VERB: The whole pan of lasagna fell off the table and *splattered* on the floor.

WEAK VERB: The first thing we did *was* pull into a parking lot and *take* an hour nap.

STRONG VERB: First, we *parked* the car in a lot and *napped* for an hour.

WEAK VERB: College *has been* a real challenge for me.

STRONG VERB: College *challenges* me.

In the next example from a research paper, the student writer is using a lot of dull verbs:

The United States *has* a law that requires schools to help all students *become* proficient in the English language. So the Office of Civil Rights *has* two concerns when it investigates school districts to evaluate equal opportunity for students with limited English proficiency (LEP). The first concern *is* whether or not the district *has* LEP students. If it *has* LEP students, then the district *has to have* a special language program. The second concern *is* to determine whether or not the district's program *is* effective in meeting students' needs.

There *are* many LEP students in the United States, but most schools *do not have* an effective way to teach them. There *are* many reasons why educators *do not have* an effective way yet. Each school *has* differing numbers of students, and there *are* many different languages spoken. For these reasons, the Office of Civil Rights does not insist that a school district adopt a particular program. Schools *have* the flexibility to choose the program they believe will best serve their students. Some of their options *are* English as a Second Language, Transitional Bilingual Education, Developmental Bilingual Education, and Structured Immersion.

This writer is relying too heavily on weak *to be* and *to have* verbs. Note how the subject comes alive with the substitution of more action-oriented verbs:

The United States *requires* schools to help all students *speak* English effectively. So the Office of Civil Rights *investigates* school districts to evaluate whether they provide equal opportunities for their students with limited English proficiency (LEP). First, it *determines* whether or not a district *contains* LEP students. If LEP students *attend* the schools in that district, those schools *must enroll* them in a special language program. Second, the Office of Civil Rights *evaluates* the effectiveness of the programs schools offer.

Many LEP students *attend* American schools, but most schools *do not teach* them well for several reasons. Each school *serves* differing numbers of students who *speak* many different languages. For these reasons, the Office of Civil Rights does not insist that a school district adopt a particular program. Instead, it *grants* schools the flexibility to choose the program they believe will best serve their students. Their options *include* English as a Second Language, Transitional Bilingual Education, Development Bilingual Education, and Structured Immersion.

Many times, the best verb for the sentence is lurking within the sentence, masquerading as another part of speech such as an adjective, noun, or adverb. Creating a more interesting sentence, then, becomes a matter of rearranging the words to put the action where it belongs, in the verb:

WEAK VERB: I had a ferocious fight with a close friend. [The best verb for this sentence—*fight*—is being used as a noun.]

STRONG VERB: I *fought* ferociously with a close friend.

WEAK VERB: I had all the clothes washed and hanging on the line to dry. [The most interesting verbs are hiding as two adjectives, *washed* and *hanging*.]

STRONG VERBS: I *washed* all the clothes and *hung* them on the line to dry.

WEAK VERB: Sparkling with color, our work was done. [The verb is disguised as an adjective.]

STRONG VERB: Our completed work *sparkled* with color.

WEAK VERB: There was a long stretch of road a mile long. [The verb hides as a noun.]

STRONG VERB: The road *stretched* for a mile.

Strong verbs are easiest to select, of course, when you're describing action, such as a story. But you can get into the habit of evaluating your verbs in everything you write, from summaries to professional reports.

In the passage from a report below, note how the subject becomes more clear and interesting simply by selecting more vivid verbs:

Dull verbs:
Video cameras *would be* less expensive to install and operate. They *could also be used* to monitor activity in all of the other buildings. After installation costs, the only other expense *would be* a person to monitor them. This *could be done* by our existing security personnel. Video cameras *are becoming* increasingly popular around the world as a form of security.

Revised for more interesting verbs:
Video cameras *cost* less to install and operate. They *could also monitor* activity in all of the other buildings. After paying installation costs, the company might *choose to spend* additional money to hire a person to monitor the system. Or existing security personnel *could perform* this task. As video cameras grow in popularity, more companies around the world *select* this form of security.

Here is another example from the work experience section of a resume:

Dull verbs:
Waited on customers, *did* daily store reports, *made* billing statements, *took* payments on accounts, and *called* past-due accounts.

Revised for more interesting verbs:
Assisted customers, *generated* daily store reports, *prepared* billing statements, *collected* payments on accounts, and *investigated* past-due accounts.

A final example comes from a memorandum:

Dull verbs:
The Internet supposedly *has* the answer to any question, but, unfortunately, it *is* not a solution for all research problems. The Internet does *have* huge amounts of information, but locating and verifying sources *can be* difficult and time-consuming. Often the information *is* just not there, or it *is* available only to those willing to pay a fee or subscribe.

Revised for more interesting verbs:
Many people *insist* that the Internet can answer any question, but, unfortunately, the Internet *cannot solve* all research problems. The Internet does *store* huge amounts of information, but users *face* a difficult and time-consuming task as they locate and verify sources of information. Often they *cannot locate* what they need, or they *discover* that only fee-paying subscribers *can access* the information.

As you try out more action-oriented verbs in your sentences, be prepared to experiment with the wording of the entire sentence. Often, it's necessary to rearrange, delete, and add other parts of speech as you search for the best action word. For example, the revised version above adds subjects (*many people, users,* and *subscribers*) to several of the sentences in order to include the best verb.

TIP:

For more about how strong verbs create effective sentences, see Chapter 3.

EXERCISE 2.3   **Verbs**

1. Rewrite the following paragraph, finding more interesting verbs for those italicized:

   Our family *had* four sons serving in the military. John *was sent* to Fort Jackson to join the 105th Engineers Combat Corps. While in the service, he *went* from a private to a lieutenant colonel, but he *was* never one to brag about his promotions. We learned about them by the titles he used in his return address on his letters to our mom. He *was* also in the Korean War in the Combat Corps of Engineers. He served his country well.

2. In the following sentences, the best verb is disguised as another part of speech. Rewrite each sentence so that a more interesting verb conveys the action:

    a.   A child abuser *has* no specific profile he has to fit.

    b.   Microsoft *has put* a lot of research and testing into their new software.

    c.   The coach's recognition of their abilities *was* a boost for the players' morale.

    d.   Epilepsy *is* a misunderstood disease throughout America.

    e.   Cupric oxide *has* a higher melting temperature and *is* a better conductor, but phosphate coating *is* cheaper and *is* more widely available for metal processing.

    f.   This county now *has* twenty-eight licensed day care centers and forty-one registered homes serving two thousand children.

    g.   Recently, Geraldo *had* an interview with a serial killer.

3.   Choose a piece of your own writing. Underline the verb in each sentence. Then revise the dull verbs to make them more interesting and action-oriented. You may have to reword all or part of your sentences.

4.   Choose a piece of your own writing that you have saved using a word processor. Use the program's "search" function to find *to be* verbs (*is, are, was, were*). Decide whether or not a more action-oriented verb could improve the sentence.

Figures of Speech

Figures of speech are the fourth type of vivid language that adds interest and clarity to writing. Metaphors, similes, and personification, three specific types of figurative language, will create images in your reader's mind to help her understand your ideas. Metaphors and similes creatively compare two things in order to reveal their similarity. Metaphors are direct comparisons, and similes are indirect comparisons that use the word *like* or *as*. For example:

Metaphors
Placed on her stomach, [a baby] will struggle to hoist her *bowling ball of a head* from the floor.[7]

Despite my most powerful efforts to regain authority over my body parts, I can only sway and stumble, a *windup monkey unhinged and unmanageable.*[8]

Similes
My prosaic feet, *like overgrown roots,* peek out from beneath the satiny folds of the perfect dress.[9]

Scattered throughout the untidy ribbon of greenery, *like a necklace of shining jewels,* were dozens of glowworms, the luminous, larval offspring of fireflies.[10]

These comparisons add descriptive interest to writing by conjuring up pictures in the reader's mind. Authors of fiction and poetry have long known the power of creative figurative language to communicate ideas while delighting the reader. For example, Pulitzer-prize winning novelist E. Annie Proulx includes some striking metaphors and similes in her book *The Shipping News*:

Every set of headlights veered into the parking lot, the glare sliding over the walls of the room *like raw eggs in oil.*

Two fishermen beside the road, lean and hard *as rifles,* mending a net in the rain . . .

A *great damp loaf of a body.* At six he weighed eighty pounds. At sixteen he was buried under a *casement of flesh.* Head shaped *like a crenshaw,* no neck, reddish hair ruched back. Features *as bunched as kissed fingertips.* Eyes the color of plastic. The monstrous chin, *a freakish shelf* jutting from the lower face.[11]

Metaphors and similes can also be included in nonfiction writing to add descriptive detail. For example, note how the passage from a student essay below is improved with the addition of a few original similes:

Shiny polyurethane plywood formed five sides of the cage, and the top was wire. I peered into the cage, scanning the floor. In one corner, a collection of tiny baby boas wiggled *like boiling spaghetti*. A combination of blood and mucus still covered the babies, which were still attached to small yolk sacs that fed them in their mother's body. The huge reptile, her markings *as clear and bold as an argyle sock* with many shades of black, tan, gray, cream, and orange, slithered gracefully around the base of the cage. When she spotted me directly above, she tried to strike.

As you attempt to include more metaphors and similes in your writing, beware of cliches. A cliche is a phrase that's no longer fresh or interesting because it has been overused; therefore, it no longer creates a picture in the reader's mind. Cliches include similes such as:

as strong as an ox

as fit as a fiddle

as slow as molasses

watched like a hawk

as busy as a bee

Instead of including dull, hackneyed phrases that everyone's heard before, strive for creativity in your comparisons. Make intriguing connections that startle or delight the reader with their originality.

Personification is a second type of figurative language that can add zest and life to your writing. To personify means to describe an inanimate or nonhuman object as though it possesses human abilities or characteristics. For example, the curtains whisper in the breeze, the fan hums, and the springs on the porch swing complain. Again, beware of cliches when you use personification. Phrases such as *waves lap the shore, wind whistles*, and *daffodils dance* are boring because they've become common.

TIP:

To find out more about techniques for discovering creative ideas, see Chapter 1.

| EXERCISE 2.4 | *Figurative Language* |

Create original, descriptive metaphors or similes for each of the following:

1. The clothes on the clothesline fluttered like _____.

2. The boy was as thin as _____.

3. The abandoned swingset was a _____.

4. The asphalt parking lot was as hot as _____.

Add a verb that personifies each of the following nouns:

5. The willow tree _____.

6. The ringing phone _____.

7. The daisy _____.

8. The truck's engine _____.

9. The fire _____.

    To sum up these sections on details, adjectives, strong verbs, and figurative language, note how the following paragraph describing a student's scuba dive in Mexico is dramatically improved when revised to include all four types of vivid language:

First version:
On a trip to Cancun, my friend talked me into going chumming. "Chum" is made up of blood and fish parts. Sharks eat it. Too late, though, I knew I didn't want to be that close to man-eaters. I opened my eyes for a moment and saw the sharks. They swam around me, eating the chum.

Revised for vivid language:
On a trip to Cancun, my friend Dan talked me into going chumming. "Chum" is a combination of the blood, heads, tails, and entrails of fish, a meal especially appealing to sharks. Chumming involves placing this stinking, gory mess in a bucket and then taking it on a scuba dive in the ocean. When you release the chum into the water, a cloud of red spreads out into the clear water, attracting sharks to the irre-

sistible scent of the blood. But seventy feet down in the chill water, after we released this foul beacon, I suddenly realized I didn't want to be that close to hungry man-eaters. But it was too late. A swarm of silvery whitetip sharks moving gracefully through the water quickly surrounded me. At least twenty of them, all three to four feet long with glassy black dots for eyes, glided above my head. Seized by fear, I trembled as I watched them open their mouths, revealing rows of jagged teeth, to gobble the chum.

This revision adds facts (the name of her boyfriend, depth of the dive, the kind of shark, the number of sharks, length of the sharks), sensory details (smell and color of the chum, temperature of the water, color of sharks' bodies and eyes), descriptive adjectives (*irresistible, foul, hungry, jagged*), strong verbs (*spreads, surrounded, glided, trembled*), and figurative language (*foul beacon*). Using more vivid language creates clearer, more interesting writing.

TIP:

> *Assemble a home reference library that includes a college-level dictionary, a thesaurus, and a grammar handbook. Keep these books nearby as you compose.*

Precise Word Choices

As you experiment with more vivid details, adjectives, verbs, and figures of speech to enliven your writing, carefully evaluate the words you choose for the meaning they convey. The English language contains over one million words, providing us with many fascinating options for communicating with others. However, this variety of choice can often increase the danger of selecting a word that does not accurately convey our intended meaning. As Mark Twain said, "The difference between the right word and the almost-right word is the difference between lightning and a lightning bug." Words have various shades of meaning that we must take into account as we search for the language to best express our thoughts.

Imprecise words will "sound" like wrong notes in a musical performance. For example, examine these sentences from students' essays:

Cigarette smokers let their smoke *run free* about the restaurant until it *infests* the lungs of innocent bystanders. [The writer has attempted to personify his subject, but the two verb choices do not accurately describe the action of cigarette smoke.]

Consummately, hiking *endows* a mental escape from life's stresses. [The word *endow* means "to provide with power or income." The writer should have simply used the more accurate *provide.* The word *consummate* cannot be changed into an adverb; even if it could, it would not fit the meaning of this sentence.]

Now look at the following passage from a letter to a newspaper editor. The italicized words are not the best choices:

A lovely sunset *pierced* through nature's *shrouds.* Twilight lingered, *spotting* the garden with a final glow. Night crept in to muffle the farmlands. The scent of flowers drifted on the breeze. Wildflowers *showed* their colorful dresses.

Imprecise word choices come in a variety of flavors. Sometimes a writer accidentally chooses the wrong word because he mistakes it for another that sounds very similar. For example: "I said some things about his formal girlfriend that weren't true" (instead of *formal*, the writer means *former*). Or, in the same vein, he might choose a homophone for his intended word choice: "Many unemployed people are idol all day" (he really means *idle*). Sometimes word choices are imprecise because they violate the tone of the rest of the piece. For instance, when we toss an informal slang term in the middle of a serious report or select a very formal word for a more conversational-sounding piece, those inappropriate words sound wrong. For example, a student writer included this statement in her research paper: "College graduates are lucky to knock down twenty thousand dollars a year." The phrase *knock down* is slang, too conversational for a formal document like a research paper. In contrast, another student, in a paragraph to a fellow student, included the sentence: "Although a lot of the information is difficult to comprehend, if you are persistent, you will prevail." This sentence (particularly the use of the word *prevail*) is too stiff and formal for a piece directed to a peer.

Another category of imprecise words includes synonyms with subtle but different shades of meaning. Consider this list of words:

boat

yacht

canoe

schooner

barge

dinghy

steamer

ferry

Though they're all modes of water transportation, they can't necessarily replace each other without significantly altering the meaning of the sentence. If you consult a thesaurus (synonym dictionary) as you write, make sure you're selecting the word from the list that most accurately reflects your meaning.

Finally, many imprecise word choices are ones the writer thought she knew, but didn't. Make sure you know the exact meaning of each word you select in order to avoid possible misunderstandings with your reader. When she wrote the following sentence in an essay, a student clearly did not know the meaning of the italicized word:

I would like to be *efficient* enough for garage mechanics to treat me like an adult, not a teenager.

Think about the mental picture an imprecise word choice can conjure up for your reader. Not only can it confuse him, but it also can leave him chuckling over a silly mental image, like this sentence from a letter to the editor:

Rolling my eyes across the dusty floor, I stretched an eyeball as it stared into the attic.

EXERCISE 2.5 *Precise Language*

Replace each of the italicized words in the passage below with a more precise choice:

I was *awestruck* when I got a speeding ticket today. I was on the *highway* in front of my *residence* when I saw the *siren* flashing behind me. I *pulled up to* the curb. A *detective* got out of his *plain* car and *hiked* up to my window. He asked me if I *comprehended* that I was *succeeding* the speed limit. I was *scandalized* by the *acquisition.* I insisted that I was *cruising* at the exact limit of thirty-five miles per hour. But then he *accursed* me of going thirty-eight miles per hour. I couldn't believe it! Only three miles per hour above the limit and this *lad* had decided that I had *perpetuated* a major *offensive.* He treated me like a *feline* and I became *infuriated.* By this time, a *mob* had gathered to watch. I argued with him, but he was *uneffected.* He *preceded* to *furnish* me with a ticket, which I *excepted* with reluctance. Then I *lamented* that I had *debated* with him. If I had treated him *respectively,* maybe he would have *let me off* with just a warning.

Chapter Summary

Clear, interesting writing always includes specific, vivid language. A reader can easily form crisp mental images of your topic when you write with **detail** (facts and sensory information), **adjectives** (descriptive words), **strong verbs** (action words), and creative **figurative language** (metaphors, similes, and personification).

The words we choose must also be precise to accurately communicate our meaning to the reader.

Suggested Writing Activities

As you write one or more of the following compositions, include sensory and factual details, action verbs, and descriptive adjectives. Also, experiment with figurative language.

1. Choose one of the following and tell the story: your most embarrassing moment, *or* a day everything went wrong, *or* a time you did something crazy.

2. Tell the story of an event or experience that changed your life.

3. Describe an interesting person you know.

4. Describe a person who has influenced your life.

5. Write directions explaining how to travel from your college's campus to your home.

6. Report on a famous historical person you have adopted as a hero or role model.

7. Write an essay explaining to a recent high school graduate why he or she should attend the college you attend.

8. Explain a problem at your workplace that causes unsafe conditions or inefficient operations.

9. Describe your dream house.

Notes

1. Mark G. Stith, "Tunnel in Time," *Southern Living* (October 1997), 113.

2. "Faculty Members and Service Providers: The Unhappy Alliance," *Disability Accommodation Digest* (Summer 1995), 4.

3. Tabitha Kenlon, "Apron Strings," *Victoria* (May 1997), 17.

4. "House Plans," *Victoria* (April 1997), 110.

5. Alex Ross, "The Musical Kaleidoscope," *The New Yorker* (August 26–September 2, 1996), 10. Reprinted by permission of the author.

6. "General Assembly Day-at-a-Glance," *The News Herald*, Morganton, N.C. (April 30, 1997), 8A.

7. Pat Wingert and Anne Underwood, "Hey—Look Out, World, Here I Come," *Newsweek Special Issue* (Spring/Summer 1997), 14.

8. Peter Swet, "The Day My World Collapsed," *Men's Health* (March 1997), 61.

9. Patricia J. Williams, "My Best White Friend," *The New Yorker* (February 26 and March 4, 1996), 97.

10. Sharon Lovejoy, "Night Life," *Country Living Gardener* (June 1997), 30.

11. E. Annie Proulx, *The Shipping News* (New York: Scribner, 1993), 2, 52, 183.

THREE

Four Rules for Clear Sentences

"I wish my writing 'flowed' better."

Many students have uttered these words, but most aren't sure what this "flow" is, or how to achieve this effect in their own compositions. Some might define it as smoothness or clarity or readability. Writing that flows is writing that does not have to be read twice, writing that doesn't get in the reader's way as he attempts to understand the ideas on the page.

So how do you achieve it in your own writing? Writing that flows is no mystery. It's determined by the way you put together words in sentences. A writer can achieve it by carefully constructing his sentences following four simple rules.

All of the examples and exercises in this chapter—those that flow and those that do not flow—come from the actual writing of students and professionals.

Rule 1: Use Strong Verbs

In Chapter 1 we discussed the importance of choosing action-oriented verbs to stimulate the reader's interest. When constructing her sentences, a writer should be aware of some common patterns that will always force her to settle for dull, weak verbs.

Avoid There Is Sentences

Any time you begin to write a sentence that starts with *There is/are/was/ were,* stop! These sentences allow the writer to rely on a weak *to be* verb, often burying the best verb choice somewhere else in the sentence. For example:

WEAK: *There was* a cold wind blowing from the North. [The best verb is hiding as an adjective, *blowing.*]

BETTER: A cold wind *blew* from the North.

WEAK: *There will* be new and better restaurants moving to our town.

BETTER: New and better restaurants *will move* to our town.

In addition to relying on a weak *to be* verb, *There is* phrases also tend to bog the sentence down with unnecessary words. We can often improve the sentence dramatically by merely deleting *there is.* In the following examples from student writing, the *there is* phrases are unnecessary. Note how each revision substitutes a better verb:

WORDY: *There is* no doubt that drugs are a main factor in the rising crime rate. [fifteen words]

BETTER: Undoubtedly, drugs *contribute* to the rising crime rate. [eight words]

WORDY: Today, *there are* many misfortunes that result in a one-parent family. [eleven words]

BETTER: Today, many misfortunes *result* in a one-parent family. [eight words]

WORDY: *There are* others like me who have rescued abused animals and found it very rewarding. [fifteen words]

BETTER: Others like me *have discovered* rewards in rescuing abused animals. [ten words]

WORDY: *There will* usually *be* a river, pond, or lake nearby that will provide many opportunities for canoeing and fishing. [nineteen words]

BETTER: Campers can *canoe* and *fish* on a nearby river, pond, or lake. [twelve words]

There is sentences are very common, and we often write too many of them because they're the first pattern we think of. Get in the habit of noticing when you write sentences that begin this way, and experiment with the wording until the verb conveys the action.

Avoid It Is *Sentences*

Sentences that begin with *It is* often suffer from the same problems—dull verbs and wordiness—that plague *there is* sentences.

WORDY: *It is* a constant battle between people for gun control and people against gun control.

BETTER: Advocates for gun control endlessly *battle* those who oppose it.

WORDY: *It's* up to the parents of the child to hire a counselor for the child.

BETTER: The child's parents *should hire* a counselor for him.

WORDY: *It is* not really getting her signature that is a problem.

BETTER: Getting her signature *does not pose* a problem.

TIP:

> *For more information about writing sentences with strong verbs, see Chapter 1.*

Avoid Passive Voice Sentences

We can write sentences using two different basic patterns. The first, called active voice, uses subject-verb-object order for the information. For example:

Joan answered the phone.
 S   V   O

This pattern, which shows the subject performing an action, is clear and direct.

The other pattern, called passive voice, flips the order, using object-verb-subject order. Using passive voice, we can rewrite the sentence above to read:

The phone was answered by Joan.
 O   V   S

Instead of a subject performing an action, passive voice contains an object having something done to it by a subject. These kinds of sentences are usually less interesting and less action-oriented because the verb is not direct. Also, we often have to read all the way to the end of the sentence before we find out who the true agent of the action really is. Note the difference between the following active and passive versions of the same sentence:

PASSIVE: The new drug is being tested by a French pharmaceutical company.

ACTIVE: A French pharmaceutical company is testing the new drug.

PASSIVE: All garbage cans will be taken to the dumpsters outside and will be emptied by the maintenance crew.

ACTIVE: Maintenance crews will take all garbage cans outside and empty them into the dumpsters.

Passive voice also tends to be ineffective because it allows us to hide the subject of the sentence. In the following paragraph from a student's essay, all four sentences are written in passive voice (italicized):

Smoking in public areas *should be prohibited.* These areas *should be maintained* in the best interest of everyone. Breathing smoke *is not desired by everyone,* so public health should outweigh the needs of an individual smoker. Smoking *should be kept* entirely within the confines of designated smoking areas.

In three out of the four sentences, the writer hides the true subject, the agent of the action. *Who* should prohibit smoking? *Who* should maintain public areas? *Who* should keep smoking confined to designated areas? The reader is left to wonder unnecessarily.

Admittedly, omitting the subject of the sentence might be acceptable in certain circumstances. For instance, sometimes it's appropriate when the subject needs to be obscured for diplomatic reasons. Examine this summary of a legislature's activities:

A bill forcing local governments to keep records of secret meetings in which taxpayer money *is promised* to private businesses ran into opposition in the Senate and *has been sent* back to a committee. The bill requires votes on incentives *to be taken* in public. Secret discussions *must be recorded,* and the records *could be released* after the deal *is completed* or fails. Opponents said making private deals public would frustrate the ability to attract industry.[1]

One final reason for avoiding passive voice: it tends to produce wordy sentences, the next rule in this chapter.

Many inexperienced writers mistakenly believe that the passive voice sounds scholarly or professional. The writer of the earlier paragraph on smoking in public places probably thought his sentences sounded sober and intelligent. On the contrary, overusing this particular pattern results in writing that is pretentious or plodding. For example, look at this passage from the minutes of a committee meeting:

The meeting *was called* to order by Joe Davis at 2:05 P.M. Bob Smith asked that the minutes *be changed* to state what *was decided* by the committee concerning Article I of the by-laws. Article I *was voted* to be changed by this committee.

The writer of this passage probably thought passive voice sentences would lend authority to this record. Instead, the passage sounds dull and stuffy.

When you occasionally write in passive voice, do it purposefully. Do not use this pattern when active voice would produce a clearer, more interesting sentence.

TIP:

For more on passive voice sentences, see page 63.

Match Subjects and Verbs

When you're experimenting with strong verbs in your sentences, make sure your subjects and verbs match. In other words, decide whether or not your subjects can actually perform the action described by the verb. In the following examples, all drawn from student writing, note the mismatch between subject (italicized) and verb (underlined), which results in a confusing or meaningless sentence:

Reckless drivers make any road hazardous, but a heavily travelled *road* already <u>obtains</u> that potential. [How can a road obtain a potential? This sentence doesn't make any sense.]

One negative *effect* of required courses <u>stems</u> from the view that students must be well-rounded thinkers. [This sentence includes too many imprecise words. How can an effect stem from a view?]

Though many popular television programs have included profanity for many years, the *degree* of this profanity <u>is becoming</u> more tasteless. [How can a degree become tasteless?]

Succeeding in math <u>contains</u> several key factors. [How can succeeding contain factors?]

The *vote* <u>was lost</u> by 27 votes. [The vote was lost by votes?]

TIP:

In an attempt to sound educated and intelligent, writers often use passive voice, complicated, wordy sentences, and huge vocabulary words. This won't make your reader think you're smart—just unclear!

Rule 2: Avoid Wordiness

The writer Pascal once penned to a friend, "I have made this letter longer than usual, only because I have not had the time to make it shorter." His statement reminds us of a paradox about writing: It actually takes more time and effort to write less. When we're trying to find the words to communicate our ideas, we usually use too many of them in our first attempt. That's fine, of course, when we're engaged in the difficult process of finding language for thoughts we've never expressed before. We should go ahead and write down the sentences as we think of them so that we can record our ideas quickly. However, *good writing always expresses an idea in as few words as possible.* We never want to make our reader wade through a lot of unnecessary words to get to our meaning. So we have to be willing to reexamine our first version and experiment with different wordings to get rid of any debris that clogs up the sentence.

WORDY: Skepticism is an attitude that is very healthy for a student to possess. [thirteen words]

BETTER: Skepticism is a healthy attitude. [five words]

WORDY: The teacher of a stop-smoking course I took (and failed) said he was told by people who were once addicted to cocaine that quitting smoking was even more difficult than giving up their drug habits. [thirty-five words]

BETTER: Former drug addicts told my stop-smoking course teacher that quitting smoking was more difficult than giving up cocaine. [eighteen words. This revision changes passive to active voice and rewords modifiers; for example, *students who were once addicted to heroin and cocaine* becomes *former drug addicts.*]

WORDY: One difference I found between the two teachers was their opinion about the students they were teaching. [seventeen words]

BETTER: The two teachers differed in their opinions about their students. [ten words. This revision eliminates a redundant modifier, *they were teaching,* and substitutes a better verb.]

WORDY: As for hunters, the wolf has been subject to a tremendous amount of animosity from them also. [seventeen words]

BETTER: Hunters also dislike the wolf. [five words]

WORDY: To pick some negative aspects of his personality would have to be first his sense of anger and bitterness. [nineteen words]

BETTER: His anger and bitterness mar his personality. [seven words]

After you compose your first draft, expect to reevaluate each sentence for possible wordiness. Many of them will need to be rearranged or pruned to better state your ideas.

COMMON WORDY EXPRESSIONS

due to the fact that	because
at this point in time	now
in the event that	if
until such time as	until
despite the fact that	although
at all times	always
in connection with	about
in view of the fact that	since
in the instance of	in

Avoid Redundant Words

As you search for wordiness in your writing, look for words and phrases that simply repeat information using different words. The italicized parts of the following sentences are redundant:

An adult understands the difference between right and wrong, *what is moral and what is immoral, what is good and what is evil.* [The italicized words merely repeat the same idea expressed by the phrase *right and wrong.*]

TV commercials are an effective sales tool *because commercials sell; and they can sell anything* from mouthwash to cars. [The italicized part is unnecessarily repetitive.]

A *reader reads* a literary analysis essay after *reading* a short story so he can get an understanding of what he *read.* [The repetition of different forms of the word *read* makes this sentence difficult to comprehend. One possible revision: One reads a literary analysis essay to better understand a short story.]

Most houses for sale are usually available to the agent that you have selected through the Multiple Listing Service, and an agent with a stable business and a solid reputation in the area usually can offer a large listing of houses available *and is also a member of the Multiple Listing Service.* [This sentence contains quite a few problems. Along with the redundant phrase, many unnecessary words are smothering the writer's idea. Verbs are also weak. One possible revision: A reputable agent can offer a large inventory of houses for sale through the Multiple Listing Service.]

After implementing the procedure *and putting it to use,* our firm saved $100,000 per year.

If you expressed an idea clearly the first time, you should not need to repeat it.

> **TIP:**
>
> *Before you include jargon (specialized language) in your writing, ask yourself if your reader will know the meanings of those terms.*

Avoid Passive Voice

Passive voice tends to produce wordy sentences. When we use the passive voice, we often write sentences that are a lot longer than they have to be.

WORDY: These walls *will have to be removed* by the contractor in order to make improvements in the actual design. [nineteen words]

BETTER: The contractor will have to remove these walls to improve the design. [twelve words]

WORDY: A survey *was distributed* to everyone on June 14, 1995, and the answers we received *were used* to determine the agenda for the next meeting. [twenty-five words]

BETTER: The Council distributed the survey on June 14, 1995, and then used its answers to determine their next meeting's agenda. [twenty words]

WORDY: There are two main points that *are argued* by people who support gun control that deal with keeping guns away from people who have no need for such powerful weapons of destruction. [thirty-two words. This sentence has many problems. It begins with *There are*, it's passive, and it's redundant.]

BETTER: Gun control advocates argue two main points. [seven words]

Arrange your sentences in the active voice pattern to avoid choking them with unnecessary words.

TIP:

For more on the passive voice, see page 57.

Rule 3: Vary Sentence Length

The sentence is the basic unit of thought within a composition. We can use one of three basic patterns to construct a sentence. Simple sentences are those with just one independent clause. Compound sentences, the second type, contain two or more independent clauses. The third type is the complex sentence, which contains both an independent and a dependent clause.

SIMPLE: Golf is definitely the most difficult sport I've ever played.

COMPOUND: I enjoy the challenge of all sports, but I especially enjoy the one that is most difficult to master.

COMPLEX: When I first watched golf on TV, I thought that hitting that little white ball would be easy.

Mature, sophisticated writing combines all three types of sentences.
We create writing that flows by mixing a variety of sentence types and
lengths.

To achieve writing that flows, avoid the two extremes when it comes
to the length of your sentences.

Avoid a Lot of Short Sentences

If your writing contains a lot of short sentences, one after another, your
reader will judge your composition to be monotonous and unsophisticated. Consider the following example from a student essay:

People walk many places all year. In the winter, people of all ages
walk at the mall. The beach is a popular place to walk in the summer.
You'll also see a lot of people just walking down city streets. In the
spring, you'll see all kinds of people walking in parks. You can walk in
the park with your dog or a friend.

Although a college student wrote this passage, it sounds as though a
third grader composed it. The short, choppy sentences are childlike and
dull.

This next example comes from a student's technical report. In this
passage, he describes aluminum signs:

They cost a little more than plastic signs. They are simple to install
either outside or inside. They do not rust like metal signs do.

These three short, simple sentences could be combined to create one
more mature sentence:

Although they cost a little more than plastic signs, aluminum signs are
simple to install either outside or inside and do not rust like metal
signs do.

This revision of three shorter sentences into one complex sentence also
helps the reader understand the relationship of the ideas better. The

addition of the subordinate conjunction *although* better establishes the contrast between the different types of signs the writer wishes to convey. This makes the revised sentence flow.

One final example comes from a book about baby care:

Most newborn babies only need a full bath three or four times a week. Every day, wash your baby's face, chin, neck, and bottom. Wash your baby's head and face first while the water and washcloth are cleanest. You do not need to use soap on the baby's face. Mild soap and water can be used on areas that need frequent washing like the baby's bottom. Rinse your baby well with the washcloth. When you are through bathing your baby, wrap her in a towel and pat dry. Rubbing irritates your baby's skin and may cause peeling.[2]

This passage consists of seven sentences, six of which are simple. This lack of variety creates a monotonous style.

However, we can combine and reorganize several of the sentences in this passage to create a more sophisticated style:

Although you should wash your baby's face, chin, neck, and bottom every day, most newborn babies need a full bath only three or four times a week. Wash your baby's head and face first while the water and washcloth are cleanest. Don't use soap on the baby's face, but do use mild soap and water on areas that need frequent washing like the baby's bottom. When you are through bathing your baby, wrap her in a towel and pat her dry because rubbing irritates your baby's skin and may cause peeling.

This revision contains four varied types of sentences: two are complex, one is compound, and one is simple.

If your writing contains a lot of short sentences, experiment with ways to combine some of them into compound and complex sentences for increased variety.

Avoid a Lot of Long Sentences

At the other extreme is the overuse of long sentences. While short sentences are monotonous and immature, too many long sentences can be rambling or confusing or pretentious. Overly long sentences try to pack too much information into one sentence. Because the purpose of a sentence is to help the reader understand separate units of thought, we defeat that purpose when we ask her to take in too much at one time. Readers can become impatient with writing that does not allow them to pause and digest thoughts in reasonable doses. The following sentence from a student's summary of a magazine article about gymnast Kerri Strug forces the reader to take in too much information:

She had to do one more vault for her team even though she was in pain because she thought the United States would lose if she didn't do the vault, but she did do it and did very well, earning 9.712, but she found out later that the United States would have won even if she hadn't done the vault.

This sentence is breathlessly wordy and unsophisticated.

Another example is from a student's descriptive essay:

His tie was green and covered with colorful cartoon characters and spread about four inches wide at the bottom and was clipped about halfway down between the knot and the end, which hung about two inches below his western style belt, and he claimed that he made the tie clip himself from a hood ornament and no one knew cars like he did.

This writer tried to link too much information together into one overly long compound sentence. The reader needs a break long before he gets one.

Rule 4: Adhere to Rules for Grammar, Spelling, and Punctuation

Standard English is defined as English that is widely used in business, academia, and the media. We expect writing we see on the job, in the classroom, and in magazines and books to conform to grammatical rules and to be spelled correctly. Readers of your writing will bring this same expectation to your compositions.

If your writing contains grammatical or spelling errors, your reader will make one or more of the following conclusions about you:

1. You did not care enough about your document to make it conform to the rules for Standard English.

2. You were too lazy to take the time to make your composition right.

3. You obviously do not know how to use Standard English, so you must be unintelligent or uneducated.

All are harsh, perhaps unfair, criticisms of you and your work. Nonetheless, readers will make these judgments if errors plague your writing. Even if your thoughts are creative or even brilliant, your reader may fail to understand or believe you if you do not express them in Standard English.

Use Proper Grammar and Punctuation

Contrary to popular belief, rules for grammar and punctuation were not devised to make your life miserable! The rules for Standard English are logical and necessary because they provide the form for expression of your ideas.

Failing to make your subjects and verbs agree or using semicolons improperly will lead the reader to form the judgments listed above. In addition, grammatical mistakes can also prevent the reader from understanding your meaning. Writing that flows is writing that doesn't get in the reader's way. But if she's constantly noticing your run-on sentences or other mistakes, she'll be distracted from the thoughts you're trying to express. She'll have to reread the sentences that contain errors, mentally correcting them so she can understand them. The following sentences all contain errors that force the reader to stop and figure out what the writer really meant:

They sent an art teacher to supervise a senior English class that has no experience with preparing a senior project. [A misplaced modifier suggests the class doesn't know what the project is, but the writer meant that the teacher doesn't know.]

Children come into the clinic with tooth decay. [A misplaced modifier says the clinic has tooth decay, but the writer meant that the children have it.]

This year's election campaign disappointed all the candidates attacked each other. [This run-on sentence forces the reader to stop, sort out where one thought ends and the next begins, and then make mental corrections before proceeding.]

Fred eats pork as much as chickens. [A parallelism error makes it sound as though the chickens eat pork.]

Grammatical mistakes, such as a usage error or a misplaced or missing comma, can also completely alter the meaning of a sentence:

They don't know *their* lines. [If the writer meant "They don't know there are lines," then he completely changed the meaning of the sentence by using *their* instead of *there are.*]

FREQUENTLY CONFUSED WORDS

None of these word pairs are synonyms. Each has its own specific definition. Do you know the difference?

advise, advice	affect, effect
loose, lose	their, there, they're
your, you're	whose, who's
it's, its	to, two, too
well, good	which, that
lie, lay	principal, principle
raise, rise	sit, set
then, than	

Write Complete Sentences

A grammatically correct sentence is always complete, which means it contains a subject and a verb and expresses a complete thought. A sentence fragment results when the writer punctuates a part of a sentence as though it were a whole sentence (with a capital letter and a period) or doesn't finish a sentence that begins with a dependent clause.

FRAGMENT WITH NO VERB: The chickens pecking in the front yard.

FRAGMENT WITH NO SUBJECT: Laughing, joking, and talking all the way.

DEPENDENT CLAUSE FRAGMENT: Standing there like a king towering over his subjects.

Correct a sentence fragment one of two ways. If the subject or verb is missing, add it and continue to let the sentence stand by itself:

The chickens pecking in the front yard *squawked* at the dog.
We laughed, joked, and talked all the way.

If the fragment is a dependent clause, attach it to the sentence that precedes or follows it:

Standing there like a king towering over his subjects, the lighthouse cast its beam into the night sky.

TIP:

> *Many word processing programs, such as Microsoft Word, will identify spelling and grammatical errors in your documents. Use them to help you edit your final draft. Don't forget, though, that spell-checkers aren't foolproof!*

Check the Spelling

Are you a good speller? Did you know that the majority of people are not good spellers? That's because spelling requires a kind of photographic

RULES FOR CLEAR SENTENCES

1. Use strong verbs.

Avoid *there is* sentences.

Avoid *it is* sentences.

Avoid passive voice sentences.

Match subjects and verbs.

2. Avoid wordiness.

Check for redundant words.

Avoid passive voice sentences.

3. Vary sentence length.

4. Adhere to rules for grammar, spelling, and punctuation.

Make sure sentences are complete.

memory. People who spell well can easily picture words in their minds; they literally "see" the word, so they know the exact order of its letters. As a matter of fact, national spelling bee champions claim to visualize words this way.

So if you aren't a good speller, you probably don't possess this type of memory. But that doesn't let you off the hook! Correct spelling is a requirement in every piece of writing you compose. If you know you don't spell well (and by now, you know), you'll have to get in the habit of checking and double-checking your spelling before sending your documents to their destinations. You can spell-check three ways. First, the old-fashioned way: Look it up in a dictionary. Second, the modern way: Use your word processor's spell-checker. And finally, ask someone who is a good speller to proofread your work and point out misspellings.

EXERCISE 3.1   *Sentences*

Determine which rules for effective sentences the following sentences are violating. Identify these rules on the line provided. Sentences 1–5 violate only one rule. Sentences 6–9 violate two different rules. Sentences 10–17 violate three different rules. Rewrite each sentence.

SAMPLE:	There is no doubt that most of our family's created problems can be solved by ourselves.
RULES VIOLATED:	1 and 2. The sentence contains weak *there is* and passive voice, both of which cause wordiness.
REVISION:	Our family can solve most of the problems we create.
SAMPLE:	When deciding on the roofing for this project, the possibility of water collecting on the top has to be taken into consideration.
RULES VIOLATED:	2 and 4. The sentence is passive, wordy, and ungrammatical.
REVISION:	The project's architects must consider the possibility of water accumulation when deciding on the best roof.

1. There are many mistakes that occur during the training of a dog. **Rule**:_____

2. After much consideration and thinking for the past couple of years, I have created a system that I think will greatly allow us to perform our duties and responsibilities in a more efficient, productive manner. **Rule:** _____

3. The physical mixture of prestressed concrete is made by combining cement, water, fine aggregates, and coarse aggregates. **Rule:** _____

4. I felt the pert, tiny leaves of the bush protruding and piercing my skin until they were embedded under it. **Rule:** _____

5. The violence and drugs that portray among the street does not help to better our young people. **Rule:**_____

6. When choosing a car that you are about to purchase, there are several things to consider. **Rules:** _____

7. I understood this poem greatly, I did not get confused with any of the ideas which were in this poem. **Rules:** _____

8. The committee representatives were reminded they would be responsible for collecting contributions from their respective departments and to make daily deposits to the business office. **Rules:** _____

9. A college diploma is a necessity in order for an employee too comply with increasing technology. **Rules:** _____

10. Her main worry is not about telling him but that she feels that it is really none of his business because it is a part of a past that should stay in the past. **Rules:** _____

11. It is said that senior citizens will no longer get social security or have their amount reduced due to the influx of elders. **Rules:** _____

12. Although there are commercials broadcast today that try to discourage drinkers from driving, these are not nearly enough to reverse all the positive messages about drinking alcohol we see. **Rules:** _____

13. Their are things more important to him then just his sports career, and that is his children and his education. **Rules:** _____

14. The lack of parental cares are another contributor to the raising crime rate due to the fact that parents are heads of the most critical organ of our society, which is the family. **Rules:** _____

15. There are numerous conclusions that can be made to explain why this software is becoming one of the populist in the world. **Rules:** _____

16. The government waists millions of dollars on welfare, they could cut those funds back, increase minimum wage, and less people would have to get welfare, therefore, saving the taxpayers' tax dollars. **Rules:** _____

17. There are large amounts of children with limited English proficiency who have educational needs that can be served by the implementation of bilingual educational methods and techniques. **Rules:** _____

Chapter Summary

You can write sentences that flow if you follow four specific rules. First, **use strong action verbs and avoid *there is, it is,* and the passive voice,** sentence constructions that all force you to settle for weak verbs. Second, **communicate your ideas in as few words as possible,** avoiding unnecessary and redundant words. Third, **alternate long and short**

sentences. And finally, **write complete sentences that adhere to the rules for grammar and spelling.**

Suggested Writing Activities

As you write one or more of the following compositions, concentrate on wording clear, concise, direct sentences.

1. Write a thank-you letter to someone who recently helped you or did something nice for you.

2. Gather information about a place where you'd like to vacation, then write a report about that place.

3. Describe an idea you have for a new invention.

4. Write a summary of a film or television show you recently enjoyed and explain why.

5. Write a memo to your current supervisor explaining how you solved a problem you faced on the job.

6. Write a letter to summarize your qualifications for a specific job.

Notes

1. "General Assembly Day-at-a-Glance," *The News Herald,* Morganton, N.C. (April 30, 1997), 8A.

2. Mary Buie et al. *Your Baby's First Year* (Raleigh, N.C.: Department of Environment, Health, and Natural Resources, 1996), 15–16.

FOUR

Complete Paragraphs

*N*ow that we've examined the kinds of words and sentences found in good writing, we'll turn in the next three chapters to the characteristics of effective paragraphs.

A paragraph can be defined as a group of sentences that develops one main idea. That idea is often stated in a topic sentence, and the other sentences in the paragraph provide the details, facts, statistics, examples, or reasons that explain and prove it.

When a paragraph is complete, it offers the reader enough information (details, facts, statistics, examples, or reasons) to help her understand and accept the main idea. Good writing contains complete paragraphs that leave no doubt about the author's meaning because they provide sufficient information. Complete paragraphs anticipate and answer all of the reader's questions and use layers of development to explain ideas.

Anticipating the Reader's Questions

As you compose, you must put yourself in your reader's shoes. As she reads about your ideas, what will she need to know? What will she want to know? A writer must try to be a mind reader as he determines what information he should communicate. Most of the time, he will not be there when his audience reads his document, so he will not be able to clarify or add to what's on the page. So he must anticipate the reader's questions and make sure he provides the answers to them as he writes. If a reader still has unanswered questions or feels that she doesn't have all of the information or examples she needs to understand the writer's ideas, then the writing is bad because it did not serve its purpose.

For example, the following paragraph attempts to explain how to cook on a barbeque grill. But the writer has left out so many important details (in brackets) that the reader doesn't have enough information to successfully complete this procedure:

To grill a hamburger, you first have to get the fire going. Remove the rack [on what?] and stack [how?] charcoal briquets [how many?] in the center of the grill. Next, squirt charcoal lighter fluid [how much?] over the briquets. Wait until the fluid soaks the charcoal [how long?]. Then toss in a lighted match. The flame will burn for a few minutes before it goes out. When this happens, let the briquets sit for awhile [how long?]. Don't squirt any more lighter fluid on the burning briquets [why?]. As the briquets get hot [how do you know they are?], spread them out with a stick so they barely touch each other [why?].

When we assume too much about the reader's level of knowledge, we risk omitting important information. The writer of the above paragraph intended to explain the procedure to someone who had never used a grill, but he assumed that his reader already knew a lot about charcoal, lighter fluid, and the grill itself. He cannot be sure the reader knows these things.

The next paragraph, which comes from a student's essay about the benefits of military service, also leaves the reader with unanswered questions:

Along with discipline and motivation, the military develops a recruit's responsibility. Young people don't want to accept responsibility for their actions. They should be free to make their own mistakes, but must also take responsibility for the consequences of their choices. Military service gives them many opportunities for learning how to do that.

The topic sentence promises that this paragraph will discuss how the military instills responsibility in its recruits. Instead, the writer goes on to offer some thoughts about responsibility in general, forgetting her original intention. Therefore, the reader is left wondering about the military's specific techniques.

The next example comes from a student's letter about the problem of homeless people in the United States, which he addressed to his senator:

One way we could aid the homeless is to stop tearing down old houses to build malls or parking lots, and rebuild or move them to create homeless shelters.

This one-sentence paragraph raises more questions than it answers. The writer needs to give his suggestion more thought, and then explain the who, what, when, where, and why of his proposal.

One final example from another student's essay also leaves the reader wondering:

Hunger is still a world problem. Many say that soy is the answer because it contains a lot of protein, but marijuana may offer an even better solution. The marijuana seed contains more protein than soy does, so it might provide a good food source for the hungry.

Upon completing this paragraph, most readers would probably want to know how the seed would be prepared, exactly how much protein it contains, and what experiments or research have led to this writer's conclusions.

Examine your own writing for places where you've tossed out general ideas without providing enough details or explanation. Readers get frustrated when they have to "fill in the blanks." And they should—that's the writer's job.

TIP:

Before writing anything, take a few moments to think about your reader. What are her goals and priorities? Why does she need this information about your topic? What might be her objections to your ideas and opinions? As you write, tailor your composition to your audience's specific needs.

Layers of Development

Paragraphs contain sentences of various levels of generality. In other words, some sentences express more general ideas, while others provide more specific information that explains those general ideas. For example, look at the following passage from a magazine:

The main problem with airlines is prosperity. The carriers find themselves flush with cash, a condition they rather like. The profits are rolling in now because of a gritty, singleminded and profoundly painful campaign of cost cutting over the past five years, in which airlines have done everything from "outsourcing" (i.e., contracting out to other firms) plane cleaning and baggage handling, to whacking travel agents' commissions, to laying off ticket agents, middle managers and mechanics, to shrinking passenger seats and eliminating meals.[1]

This paragraph begins with a general idea by using the word *prosperity* to describe the current condition of airlines. But *prosperity* is an abstract term, one that means different things to different people, so the writer adds another sentence to explain what he means. The phrase *flush with cash* in the second sentence is a specific development (or explanation) of the first sentence; it defines the term *prosperity*. Then the third sentence explains how the airlines became *flush with cash*, so it further develops the idea in the second sentence. Each sentence in this example, then, is more specific than the one before.

We can visually demonstrate this relationship between the sentences by lining them up according to how general or specific they are:

| | |

The main problem with airlines is prosperity.

| The carriers find themselves flush with cash,

| a condition they rather like.

| | The profits are rolling in now because

| | of a gritty, singleminded and profoundly

| | painful campaign of cost cutting over the

| | past five years . . .

| | |

It's helpful to think of imaginary margin lines that indicate how general or specific a sentence is. The most general statement is the first one, so we place it at the left margin line. The second sentence further develops the first, so we indent it to indicate that it's more specific. We align the third sentence with a third imaginary margin line to show that it provides more information to explain the second sentence. The more specific sentences are subordinate to the general topic sentence.

The relationships of general and specific sentences will vary depending on the paragraph. This next passage from a book develops ideas using a different pattern:

| | | |

Not every adverse reaction to a food or other substance,

however, is an allergy.

| *In fact,* in some studies of children, specialists

| were able to confirm allergy in fewer than half

| the subjects—all of whom had been previously

| diagnosed as "allergic."

| | What appears to be an allergy may sometimes

| | be an enzyme deficiency.

| | | Children with insufficient levels of

| | | the enzyme lactase, *for example,* are

| | | unable to digest the milk sugar

| | | lactose, and thus react badly to milk

| | | and milk products.

| | | *And* those with celiac disease are

| | | unable to digest gluten, a substance

| | | found in many grains, and thus appear

| | | to be allergic to those grains.

| | | The workings of an immature digestive

| | | system or such common infant problems

| | | as colic may *also* be misdiagnosed as

| | | allergy.[2]

| | | |

In this paragraph, the last three sentences are all specific examples of the enzyme deficiency mentioned in the third sentence. That's why we line them up along the fourth margin line to indicate that they all equally develop that third sentence. They are all coordinate, or equal, to each other.

Good writing includes **clue words** that help the reader understand the subordinate and coordinate relationships between sentences. Words such as *and, also, too, first, second, third, but, however,* and *in other words* indicate coordinate relationships. These words signal that this sentence is equal to one that preceded it. Words such as *for example* and *for instance* indicate subordinate relationships. Also, adjectives such as *this* and *that* and pronouns such as *he, she,* and *they* often reveal subordinate relationships by referring to something that came before. These kinds of words help the reader see that the sentence is more specific than the one that preceded it. In the paragraph about allergies above, the clue words are italicized.

> **TIP:**
>
> *For more about clue words, see the section about transitions in Chapter 5.*

In the next passage from a student's report on a day care center, the general-specific relationships of the sentences follow a different pattern:

| | |

The day care facility's director must obtain certain information from parents who wish to enroll their child.

| *First,* she must get the child's full name and
| birth date, a list of the child's allergies, and a copy
| of the child's immunization record.
| *Second,* the director should obtain information
| about the child's parents.
| | *This* information should include both parents'
| | names, home phone number, places of
| | employment, work phone numbers, and
| | medical insurance.
| *Third,* the parents must complete an emergency
| care form.
| | On *this* card, the parents should write the
| | name and phone number of the child's
| | doctor, the name and phone number of the
| | child's dentist, the name of the preferred
| | hospital, and a list of people who can be
| | contacted in an emergency.
| *Finally,* the director should obtain general information
| about the child's playing, eating and sleeping
| habits, fears, and likes and dislikes.

| | |

The sentences we include to explain more general ideas are called **layers of development.** As you write each sentence, ask yourself, "Is there an idea in this sentence that I should explain further or give an example for?" If there is, add another "layer," another sentence that clarifies the more general idea that preceded it.

Mature, sophisticated writing includes many rich layers of development. For example, look at this paragraph from a magazine, which contains four layers:

| | | | |

Extreme sports are not quite *that* dangerous.

But the possibility of physical harm is very real.

| For the most extreme athletes, busted body parts are a
| fact of life: In-line skating alone sent 105,000
| people to the emergency room in 1995, many with
| fractured bones resulting from the sport's frequent
| body-meets-pavement collisions.

| | [X Games athlete T. J.] Lavin, who ruptured his
| | spleen and cracked several ribs in an accident
| | a few years ago, says with a smile, "Man, I've
| | busted my head open so many times I've lost
| | count."

| In the more outlandish disciplines, the Grim Reaper
| elbows his way into the equation.

| | Frank Gambalie, *for example,* an expert BASE
| | jumper, is matter of fact about the risks he
| | faces while pursuing a sport that has claimed
| | 39 lives: "There aren't many injuries in BASE
| | jumping. You either survive or you die."

| | Ice climbing, despite its innocuous name, *also*
| | ranks particularly high on the danger list.

| | | Death is always just around the corner
| | | when you're scaling ice walls with a
| | | pair of pickaxes.

| | | | Says Nancy Prichard, a prominent
| | | | ice climber: "I expect to lose
| | | | three to four friends a year."[3]

| | | | |

Bad writing includes very few layers of development; if you were to rearrange it as we have the paragraphs above, it would probably contain about two levels of development. Consequently, because it's not specific enough, it leaves the reader wondering what the writer really means.

For example, examine the following paragraph from a student's report:

My oldest brother and I don't communicate very well. Our nine-year age difference contributes to the problem, but *we believe differently about everything.* The only exception is our *taste in sports teams.* Otherwise, we live *very different life-styles.*

The italicized phrases are general statements that need to be further explained. Layers of development should clarify *what* specific beliefs are different, *which* specific teams they both like, and *how* their lifestyles differ. Because we don't get these explanations, we still don't know much more about the writer's relationship with his brother than we did before we read this paragraph.

The next example, from a student's essay arguing against smoking in public, also lacks layers:

Smoking in public affects *everyone.* Second-hand smoke is as *damaging* as first-hand, especially for *infants* and *asthma patients.*

This paragraph lacks specific data to prove the idea of smoking as "damaging." This writer needs to add facts, statistics, or anecdotes to explain how and why smoking is dangerous. Then she needs to explain how it specifically affects infants and asthma patients.

Another example from a student's research paper also contains phrases that need to be clarified with specific examples:

The *length and structure of the school day* for severely handicapped students should equal that for nonhandicapped students. *School facilities and resources* should be equally accessible to all. As much as possible, *transportation* for handicapped students should equal *transportation* for nonhandicapped students.

We could improve this paragraph by adding additional layers, along with a few clue words to help the reader follow the relationships between the sentences:

The length and structure of the school day for severely handicapped students should equal that for nonhandicapped students. If a regular school day lasts seven hours, then it should last seven hours for the handicapped student. If nonhandicapped students attend six different classes, then the handicapped student should attend six classes, too. *Also,* school facilities and resources should be equally accessible to all. *For example,* handicapped students should be able to use all restrooms and water fountains, as well as the library, gymnasium, and cafeteria. *Finally,* as much as possible, transportation for handicapped students should equal transportation for nonhandicapped students. If a non-handicapped student rides a school bus for thirty-five minutes every morning, *for instance,* then his handicapped neighbor should ride that same bus.

TIP:

Some layers of development consist of information you discover through research, such as facts, statistics, quotations, and expert testimony.

The following example from a student's essay is arranged to show where ideas need to be further developed:

| | | |

Americans are still guilty of race discrimination.

| Many still judge people according to skin color and appearance.

| | [Give an example or anecdote from your own

| | experience.]

| Parents teach their children to be prejudiced.

| | [How?]

| | Kids model their parents' behavior.

| | | [Give an example or anecdote from

| | | your own experience.]

| Television shows and movies portray racism as humorous.

| | [Give some specific examples of shows

| | and movies that do this.]

| | | |

The writer offers a thorough second layer of development (all of the particular ways that race discrimination is problematic); however, he stops short of providing the specific examples that would clarify what he means. Note also the absence of clue words that could help the reader understand coordinate and subordinate relationships.

Another example comes from a memorandum:

| | |

Employees who participate in this program will benefit in several ways.

| They will develop leadership and interpersonal

| skills by completing a special training program and

| participating in activities throughout the year.

| | [What specific skills? What kind of

| | activities?]

| They will meet and interact with community leaders

| through close contact with the public relations office.

| | [Give examples of leaders they might

| | meet.]

| Also, they will earn a bonus for each

| year they participate in the program.

| | [How much?]

| | |

This writer should have added a third layer of development to give examples of each general statement.

Additional layers are also needed in this next paragraph from a student's essay:

| | | |

Golfers play on wide, grassy areas called courses.

| These courses often nestle against woods, rivers,

| creeks, or lakes.

| | [Give an example of a specific course.]

| Some of the most beautiful courses are near

| the ocean.

| | [Give some examples, along with more

| | details to describe their beauty.]

| Many golf courses are further enhanced by

| lovely homes lining the fairways.

| | [Give examples of specific courses.]

| | | Golf allows you to enjoy a beautiful

| | | environment, as well as the challenge

| | | of the game itself.

| | | |

Even professional writing sometimes lacks adequate layers of development:

| | |

About 40 percent of people who need to make a change are

at [the precontemplation] stage, says [psychologist James]

Prochaska.

| They may be unaware that a habit is hazardous.

| | [Give an example, such as cigarette smoking

| | or overeating.]

| Or, they may know that it's unhealthy, but not

| admit of a personal need to change.

| | [Tell about a specific person you know who

| | feels this way.]

| Or, they may be discouraged by previous failures

| and believe that such problems are beyond their

| control.[4]

| | [Tell about a specific person you know

| | who feels this way.]

| | |

All of these writers stopped at the second layer of development, and thus presented ideas that are only half-explained.

A final example from a student's literary analysis also lacks layers of development:

| | | |

Chaucer's *Troilus and Criseide*, completed about 1385,

adapts the story of Boccaccio's *Il Filostrato*.

| Chaucer's main character is an Englishwoman.

| | [Who is she? What's her name?]

| | She is round, not flat, which gives her more

| | substance than her counterpart in Boccaccio's

| | version.

| | | [Explain how the character is "round"

| | | and then further elaborate on how

| | | Boccaccio's version is different.]

| | | |

To ensure that you are including sufficient layers of development in your own writing, try the following techniques:

1. When you compose your first draft, you may want to arrange your sentences along imaginary margin lines in order to evaluate how many layers of development you're including. Doing so will also remind you to review each sentence for any thoughts that need further clarification.

2. Count the sentences in your paragraphs. While there is no magic maximum or minimum number, your paragraphs are probably not adequately developed if they contain only three or four sentences each.

3. Scan your drafts for the phrase *for example*. This phrase often begins sentences that really help your reader grasp your ideas. If you never begin sentences this way, you may not be including the information

in the form of specific instances or anecdotes that your reader will need in order to understand you.

Layers of Development

1. Rearrange the following paragraphs along imaginary margin lines to show the general-specific relationships between the sentences. Underline all of the clue words that help you determine coordinate and subordinate relationships.

Example:

With Tiger [Woods] there was never any guesswork. I knew how much he could take. So I pulled every nasty, dirty, obnoxious trick on him week after week. I dropped a bag of clubs at impact of his swing. I imitated a crow while he was stroking a putt. When he was about ready to hit a shot, I would toss a ball right in front of his, and it would cross his line of vision. I would make sure I stood in his line of sight and would move just as he was about to execute the shot. I would cough as he was taking the club back. I would say, "Don't hit it in the water." Those were the nice things I did. In other words, I played with his mind.[5]

Rearranged into layers of development:

| | | |

With Tiger [Woods] there was never any guesswork.

I knew how much he could take.

| So I played every nasty, dirty, obnoxious

| trick on him week after week.

| | I dropped a bag of clubs at impact of his swing.

| | I imitated a crow while he was stroking a putt.

| | When he was about ready to hit a shot, I would

| | toss a ball right in front of his, and it would

| | cross his line of vision.

| | I would make sure I stood in his line of sight

| | and would move just as he was about to execute

| | the shot.

| | I would cough as he was taking the club back.

| | I would say, "Don't hit it in the water."

| | | *Those* were the nice things I did.

| | | *In other words,* I played with his mind.

| | | |

a. A few simple changes in your kitchen can prevent many cases of food poisoning. Wash everything that comes into contact with raw meat—including cutting boards, knives, platters, and your hands—with hot water and soap. Make sure meats and eggs are well-cooked. Rinse raw fruits and vegetables thoroughly in cold water, and store cooked and raw foods separately. Refrigerate meat, eggs and other perishable food immediately.[6]

b. There have always been color crazes, historically brought on by mere availability. In the early 1800s, bright yellows were popularized by the introduction of chromate and cadmium pigments, a development that greatly affected the painting of J. M. W. Turner. Likewise, the Impressionists made generous use of the new blues and greens that emerged in their day. In this century, novelty gave way to marketing as manufacturers came to shape public tastes in color. In 1934, for instance, the American Tobacco Co. found that women wouldn't buy Lucky Strikes because the then green box clashed with their clothes. The solution: make green hot. In short order, the company set up a "color-fashion bureau," underwrote a green-themed society ball, enlisted magazine editors and bought off French couture houses. By year's end hordes of newly sensitized women started buying Lucky Strikes packs as fashion accessories.[7]

c. We have placed two trash cans near your desk, one for recyclable paper and one for regular trash. Use the largest can for recyclables and the smaller can for nonrecyclables. Recyclable paper includes white, colored, glossy, mail, card stock, folders, etc. Nonrecyclables include carbon paper, tissue, napkins, paper plates, paper cups, paper towels and food wrappers.

d. The Kaizen teamwork method offers distinct advantages. By using this approach, a company can increase production, improve employees' morale, and significantly reduce operating costs. One example is a project that Boom Dynamites finished in 1994. Their goal was to reduce the wash scrap at the ITT automotive plant in Morganton. The team investigated the problem and then created a training procedure for new employees, who were responsible for the high scrap output. After implementing the new procedure, the company saved $100,000 per year.

2. Select three paragraphs from reports or essays you've written. Arrange them into layers of development.

3. The following all lack adequate layers of development. Insert sentences (layers) to explain or give examples for the *highlighted* phrases.

a. Jones High School was a melting pot of people with *different cultures, backgrounds, lifestyles, and personalities.* I *learned to accept* people who were different from me.

b. *Parents' indifference* contributes to the rising crime rate. When the heads of the family *neglect their responsibilities,* their children end up with *people who will lead them astray,* even encouraging them to commit *crimes.*

c. Ask *open-ended questions* [to break the ice with a stranger]. You'll get a *longer response* than a simple yes or no to keep the conversation flowing.[8]

d. I am attending college to increase my skills, to build my self-esteem, and to gain the necessary credentials for today's jobs.

   Postsecondary education will give me skills and training for my future.

   Education also helps me get to know myself. It encourages me to explore who I am.

   Finally, most of today's jobs require a college degree. Companies want people who have proven they can learn by completing a program of study. Without a college degree, you often won't be hired.

   Furthering my education will make me better off for the future.

Chapter Summary

To help the reader understand your ideas, anticipate and answer all of her questions. Adding **layers of development**—examples and explanation—will provide the specific information the reader will need to comprehend your more general statements. When you include several layers, along with **clue words** to indicate relationships between your sentences, you will write paragraphs that fully explain your ideas.

Suggested Writing Activities

As you write one or more of the following compositions, include at least three layers of development in each of your paragraphs.

1. Write a fan letter to an actor, musician, or author you admire.

2. Write a letter to a friend or relative explaining either your current job responsibilities or the classes you're taking.

3. Choose a hobby or sport in which you participate, then do one of the following: report on one of your favorite experts in the field, *or* explain the benefits of engaging in this activity, *or* explain all of the materials or equipment a person needs to begin participating in this activity.

4. Report on an innovative technique or product in your field of study.

5. Propose some fundraising projects for an organization to which you belong.

Notes

1. S. C. Gwynne, "Flying into Trouble," *Time* (February 24, 1997), 46.

2. Arlene Eisenberg et al., *What to Expect the First Year* (New York: Workman Publishing, 1989), 232.

3. Brendan I. Koerner, "Extreeeme," *U.S. News and World Report* (June 30, 1997), 53, 56. Copyright ©1997 U.S. News and World Report. Used by permission.

4. Nick Gallo, "Challenge to Change," *Better Homes and Gardens* (January 1997), 44.

5. Earl Woods, "What I Taught Tiger," *USA Weekend* (April 18–20, 1997), 8.

6. Susan S. Lang, "Stomach Trouble?" *Woman's Day* (June 24, 1997), 56.

7. Gary Trudeau, "Hues You Can Use," *Time* (January 27, 1997), 67.

8. Kerith McElroy and Janet Sobesky, "The Do-Anything-Better Guide," *Woman's Day* (July 15, 1997), 59.

Coherent Paragraphs

*I*n addition to being complete, effective paragraphs must also be coherent. *Coherent* means that the paragraph makes sense because it offers a clear progression of thought. In other words, the reader can easily follow the writer's ideas from sentence to sentence.

We achieve coherence in our paragraphs in two ways: First, we use methods of development to explain and develop our ideas; and second, we use transitions to help the reader understand the relationships between our sentences.

Methods of Development

Chapter 4 discussed layers of development, which are the facts, data, statistics, details, examples, and anecdotes that a writer uses to explain and develop general ideas or abstract concepts. In this chapter, we'll examine some common patterns for arranging these layers to achieve coherence. These patterns, called "methods of development," are easily recognized by readers, so they're effective for explaining your ideas.

The next sections give examples of the most common development methods: narration, description, exemplification, process analysis, comparison and contrast, cause and effect, division, classification, and reasons. These methods can be combined in one paragraph (as we'll see later); however, we'll first look at each method in isolation.

Topic sentences in each paragraph are underlined. Where no topic sentence is underlined, the main idea is implied, rather than directly stated.

Narration

One way to develop an idea stated in a paragraph's topic sentence is to tell a story to explain or illustrate it. For instance, the following passage from a book makes a statement about young children, then narrates an experience of one particular child to prove that statement:

This talent [for practical smartness] can be seen in younger children as well. For instance, a television news story reported on a five- or six-year-old child whose mother was epileptic. She had a seizure just as she was about to get into the shower, and was lying unconscious in the tub with scalding water pouring over her. There was no one else in the house but the little boy, who called 911 and gave the dispatcher directions to his house. But the thing that really was impressive was that before calling 911, the boy turned on the cold-water tap full force to keep his mother from being even more badly burned. He had tried to turn off the hot-water tap, but it was too hot to touch.[1]

In this next example from a student's essay, the writer also tells a story:

I never realized how little self-confidence I had until I attended a seminar about self-esteem. In one group activity, we rated our strengths and weaknesses. When we finished our own lists, we had to rate the co-workers in our group. My co-workers rated my self-confidence as very low. They said I was incapable of saying no to them if I didn't have time to help. They confessed that they didn't have much respect for someone who couldn't speak up for herself, and they said they'd like me just as much if I was more assertive.

A final example is from a magazine article:

Of nine significant Korean Air accidents in the past 20 years, some evidence of pilot error surfaced in seven. "There is a pattern of misconduct by pilots," charges Steve Pounian, a New York City lawyer who represented some of the families in the shooting down of Flight 007. Some of the errors are egregious. The Korean Air cargo pilot responsible for an accident in Anchorage in 1983 committed an almost farcical series of mistakes. Refusing to ask for directions in a snowstorm, he taxied onto the wrong runway and eventually took off in the wrong direction, clipping a commuter plane as he lifted off. Both aircraft were destroyed, though no one died. Alaska's Supreme Court upheld a lower-court decision blaming the Korean pilot for "willful misconduct." His conduct was also stupid; the court said he "followed tracks in the snow that he assumed were left by other aircraft."[2]

In the above paragraph, the story of one particular airplane crash illustrates the idea that many air accidents occur because of the pilot's errors.

Description

Sometimes, we need to give descriptive details to explain an idea. These details might include size, weight, dimensions, color, materials of construction, parts, and so on. For example, this paragraph from a report on a day care center helps the reader visualize the playground area by providing details about its dimensions and the various equipment and structures it contains:

The layout of this playground is designed for three activities: playing, eating, and storing supplies. The play area will include swings, a slide, monkey bars, and an open area for playing games such as kickball and dodge ball. The picnic area will be furnished with six picnic tables, which can seat up to forty children at a time. A 150-square-foot, locked building will store supplies and equipment. The entire playground will measure fifty feet by eighty feet and be enclosed by a four-foot-high chain-link fence.

Another example, from a student's essay, describes a person:

Aunt Maud had silver-gray hair and a face creased with deep wrinkles. Her blue eyes twinkled behind metal-framed glasses, which perched atop her long nose. She was almost always smiling.

In this passage, the writer provides details about the subject's physical appearance and personality traits to help us understand what she's like.

A final example comes from a catalog advertising jewelry boxes for sale:

Intricate, three-dimensional designs in pastel shades of pink, green and blue are highlighted with faux pearls and golden accents. Select from the romantic Cherub or Doves design. Made of durable cold-cast ceramic with beautiful details, each measures 8 1/4" × 5 1/2" × 3". Interior features a lift-out tray and foam rolls lined in off-white felt. Perfect for storing chains, earrings and rings. Inside the hinged, molded lid is a mirror. Tray measures 6 3/4" × 3 3/4" × 1".[3]

This description of an object helps us visualize the subject by providing details about its appearance, dimensions, and materials of construction.

TIP:

For longer assignments, divide the writing task into stages instead of trying to complete the whole project all at once. Break it down into planning, fact-finding, organizing, writing, and revising, then set deadlines for the completion of each step with breaks built in between. Use a calendar to record the date the final product is due. A few days prior to that, schedule a date to complete the rough draft. A few days before that date, set a deadline for creating an organization plan. Spread the entire procedure over a longer period of time, and stick to your smaller goals according to schedule.

Exemplification

Some general ideas are best developed by presenting specific examples that illustrate the main point. For instance, read this passage from a magazine article:

<u>With your desire recognized, your belief firmly in place and your goal clearly identified, the next step is to visualize yourself going for the goal</u>. Runners envision themselves in the starting blocks, exploding smoothly at the sound of the gun, moving to their favorite position in the pack, accelerating, passing the leaders, bursting through the tape the winner. They run the race over and over in their minds with the greatest clarity, as though they were watching a videotape.[4]

This paragraph uses runners as one example of people who succeed by using visualization.

The next example comes from a student's literary essay:

<u>The Puritans believed in signs and omens</u>. One example comes from William Bradford's account of their voyage to New England. During the trip, a sailor who laughed at the Pilgrims suddenly fell ill and died. Bradford claimed that God punished the man for being rude to His chosen people. This omen indicated God's favor toward the Pilgrims. Also during this voyage, a young Puritan named John Howland almost died when a storm swept him overboard. However, "it pleased God" to rescue him so he could become "a profitable member of the church." Bradford interpreted this event to mean that God would pro-tect those who wished to serve Him.

This author selected one particular Puritan and chose examples from his writing to illustrate the group's belief in omens.

A final example is from a book:

<u>Sometimes even so-called mentally retarded people have tremendous practical skills</u>. They have to in order to get through life. For example, one study described a mentally retarded man who, unable to tell time, walked around wearing a broken watch. When he needed to know the time, he would ask someone, pointing out that his own watch was broken.[5]

This paragraph offers one specific individual as an example to illustrate the idea in the topic sentence.

Process Analysis

Process analysis can be either directive or informational. **Directive process analysis** gives the reader how-to instructions (directions) so that she can recreate a procedure herself. For example, you could explain the steps for making a cake or for changing the oil in your car. **Informational process analysis** explains a process so that the reader can understand how something is done or how something works. For instance, you might explain how bees make honey or how an air traffic control tower works.

This paragraph from a magazine article is an example of directive process analysis:

Stress-induced fatigue can be dispelled by some simple stretching, says clinical psychologist Robert Gatchel. Stand up, raise your arms over your head with your fingers locked and push towards the ceiling. Gently stretch to each side and then push back as far as you can. Next, try stretching out your neck and shoulders by rotating your head in a circle, first to the right, then to the left.[6]

The author gives step-by-step directions for the reader to follow.

This passage from a memo also offers a directive process analysis:

Please observe the following rules to keep the workout room running smoothly:

1. If others are using the equipment too, work on the machines in order. If you have to leave the circuit, don't cut in front of someone else.

2. Don't socialize while others are in the circuit. One benefit of circuit-type training is continuous exercise without long breaks. Move aside to chat and let others continue.

3. If you want to do more repetitions than the recommended maximums (12 upper, 15 lower) on a particular machine, please return to

that machine later when you won't interfere with others moving in the circuit.

4. The stationary bicycles, cross country ski machine, treadmills, and rowing machines are not part of the circuit. Use them at the beginning or the end of your overall workout.

Like the previous example, this passage also provides directions.

This last paragraph from a magazine is an example of informational process analysis:

How could plants worsen global warming? The culprits, says biologist Jim Collatz of NASA's Goddard Space Flight Center, are the tiny pores called stomata on leaf surfaces. Stomata allow carbon dioxide to seep into leaves, where it is used in photosynthesis, and they also let water out. Normally, when the sun heats up a plant water inside the plant gets warm and evaporates out the stomata. But to cut down on water loss, stomata close when a leaf has absorbed enough carbon dioxide, and as carbon dioxide concentration goes up, they stay closed for longer periods of time. With stomata closed, hot water inside the plant can't escape. The water heats the plant, and the plant in turn warms its surroundings. So the sun's energy, instead of being used to evaporate water from vegetation, heats plants—and the rest of the planet.[7]

This passage describes the steps of a process so the reader can understand the main point.

Comparison and Contrast

Sometimes we need to develop an idea by showing how two or more subjects are alike or different. **Comparison** involves examining the similarities between two subjects, while **contrast** explores the subjects' differences. A paragraph might do one or the other or both to explain a point to the reader.

The following example from a newspaper article includes both comparison and contrast:

<u>Downy and hairy woodpeckers are very similar</u>. Their patterns are almost identical, checkered and spotted with black and white with black backs, but the downy has a small bill while the hairy has a long one. The downy is smaller than the hairy as well. Males of both species have small red patches on the backs of their heads. Downy and hairy woodpeckers are unique because they are the only woodpeckers with white backs. Other woodpeckers may have white bars on their backs, or white rumps, but not white backs.[8]

This paragraph presents the similarities (patterns and backs) of the two woodpeckers and also discusses their differences (size of bill and overall size).

Another example, which comes from a student's report, uses contrast only:

Though gravel is less expensive than concrete, it will erode and require periodic replacement. Concrete may cost more initially, but it lasts longer than gravel and requires little maintenance. Maintenance costs for gravel are higher because you have to pay for labor, too. Concrete may require labor for filling cracks now and then, but it's still cheaper than the cost of constant gravel maintenance.

This passage discusses only the three main differences (cost, durability, and maintenance) between gravel and concrete; therefore, it contrasts the two types of materials.

One last example is this next paragraph about professional baseball umpires, which comes from an essay published in a magazine:

Fearing retaliation from the men in blue, nobody in baseball will say a critical syllable on the record. <u>Many players and managers believe that American and National League umpires are different and that the Nationals are generally better</u>. They call a bigger strike zone (although not as big as the rule book defines it), hustle more to be in position and keep a better grip on the game. However, one veteran of many seasons says: "If you question a ball-and-strike call of a National League umpire, the next pitch, if it's catchable, is a strike." Sometimes in both leagues a punitive call is communicated to a player in advance: "If you think that last call was bad, wait till you see the next one."

And sometimes the punitive call is made with an emphasis clearly intended to provoke the player. Such behavior degrades a contest.[9]

This paragraph uses both comparison and contrast, first explaining how National and American League umpires are different, and then stating how they are alike.

> *In addition to reference books, the people you know can be valuable sources of assistance as you write. Many of your family, friends, fellow students, and co-workers may have the skills and knowledge to help you with everything from getting ideas to proofreading for spelling and grammatical errors.*

Cause and Effect

Another way to develop ideas is to give the reasons why something occurred (examining **causes**), or to explain the consequences of something (exploring **effects**). Using the cause and effect method of development often requires the writer to present a chain reaction of events and explain how one thing led to another. For example, read this paragraph from a book:

What we have seen is that low test scores set in motion a chain of events that can lead to poor later outcomes, independent of the abilities tests measure. Once a child is labeled as stupid, his opportunities start to dry up, and forces in the environment conspire to lead to the outcomes that would be expected and appropriate for a stupid person. Teachers expect less. Placements in lower tracks, reading groups, or, later, colleges reflect the reduced expectations. Good work is viewed with suspicion: Maybe the individual cheated, or at least got outside help. Labels are not just descriptions of reality; they contribute toward shaping reality.[10]

This passage clearly explains how a child's low test scores lead to a series of negative consequences, or effects.

This next example, from a student's essay, discusses both causes and effects:

When I was only four years old, two policemen woke my mom, my two brothers, and me with the news that my father was killed in a one-car accident. He was drunk and ran into a tree. <u>My dad's alcohol-related death influenced my decision to not drink</u>. I decided I would never hurt my loved ones as my dad's death hurt me. Now I avoid regular drinkers and their parties. Some people tease me about my decision, but I don't care. My close friends respect and support my choice.

Not only does the writer explain the reason he made the decision not to drink, he goes on to examine the effects of that decision.

A final example from a student's report focuses on effects only:

<u>Old-growth forests can be improved with select-cutting, a procedure that benefits both the remaining plant and tree life and also the wildlife</u>. Trees need to be thinned out because the dense canopy of leaves darkens the forest floor, preventing seedlings from growing. Old uncut trees left to die will eventually fall, leaving rotting stumps and decaying logs. This debris can choke small streams, slowing the flow of water.

In the passage above, the writer traces the chain reaction of events that results from failing to select-cut trees in a forest.

Division

Some ideas are best developed by explaining how something can be divided into smaller parts. Often, it's easier to understand a larger entity or concept by breaking it down into its components and examining each in detail. This first example is from a student's essay:

<u>The summer Olympics is composed of many exciting events</u>. One of the main events is diving, which includes both platform and springboard

diving. Another popular event is swimming. Two types of swimming races are the backstroke and the butterfly stroke. Track and field contests include bicycle races, sprints, marathons, and relay races. One other event is gymnastics. Women gymnasts compete on the parallel bars, the balance beam, the vault, and the floor exercise.

This passage divides a subject into its separate parts to help us better understand that subject.

Another example comes from a student's essay:

<u>Alcohol damages the liver in three stages</u>. During the first stage, the liver becomes fatty, but no symptoms appear. Abstinence can reverse this damage. The second stage is hepatitis, or inflammation. If drinking continues, the liver enlarges, causing pain. Cirrhosis is the third and most advanced stage of liver disease. Scar tissue replaces working liver cells. If untreated, cirrhosis is fatal.

This writer helps us understand the effects of alcoholism by identifying three distinct stages of liver damage.

One last example comes from a book:

The period in English literature generally called the *Renaissance* is usually considered to have begun a little before 1500 and to have lasted until the Commonwealth Interregnum (1649–1660). <u>It consisted of the Early Tudor Age (c. 1500–1557), the Elizabethan Age (1558–1603), the Jacobean Age (1603–1625), and the Caroline Age (1625–1642)</u>. In the early period, English authors felt the impact of classical learning and of foreign literatures, together with some release from church authority. The New World was transforming England into a trading nation no longer at the periphery of the world but at its crossroads. During the reign of Elizabeth, England became a world power; its drama and its poetry attained great heights in the work of such writers as Spenser, Sidney, Marlowe, and Shakespeare. By the time that James came to the throne, a reaction was beginning to set in, expressed through a growing cynicism, a classical dissatisfaction with the extravagance and unbounded enthusiasm of the sixteenth century, a tendency toward melancholy and decadence. At the same time, as though in reaction

to this reaction, there was a flourishing of baroque elements in literature. As the conflict of Puritan and Cavalier grew in intensity, these
elements grew also. And by the time Charles lost his head, the
Puritanism that was itself a major outgrowth of the intense
individualism of the Renaissance had spelled an end to most of its
literary greatness.[11]

The paragraph above helps us better understand this literary movement
by dividing it into four different periods and then briefly describing
each one.

Classification

Classification places things in groups based upon qualities or characteristics they share. When we explain an idea with the classification
method, we demonstrate how the subject can be thought of in
terms of categories. For example, study this passage from a magazine
article:

It's perfectly normal for kids to exhibit a certain behavioral style in
class. Behavior, after all, is a primary form of communication for
school-age children. Decipher its meaning and you'll be better
equipped to help your child succeed academically. <u>Here are a few of
the more common classroom styles</u>: *The class clown* tends to be an
outgoing, gregarious child in need of attention. At home he's also
charming and funny, but at times drives you crazy with his endless
capacity for high jinx. *The shrinking violet* is shy, introverted and insecure about speaking up in school. In a comfortable setting at home or
with close friends, however, she may be full of talk. *The daydreamer*
who tunes out or doodles in class may have a concentration problem,
or the work could be either too advanced or too easy. *The eager
beaver* tends to be a high achiever who's naturally motivated. But he
can be hard on himself if he doesn't meet his own standards.[12]

This paragraph groups children into one of four categories depending on
their classroom behaviors.
    Another example comes from a student's report:

<u>Plant life thrives in this forest</u>. Various species of wildflowers grow in sunny patches. These flowers include mountain laurel, jewelweed, daisies, blackberries, ginseng, and strawberries. Ferns are another category of plant life. Eighteen different types of fern species are native to this region.

This passage categorizes both wildflowers and ferns.

One last example is from a student's research paper:

<u>Child abuse can be characterized as physical, emotional, or sexual</u>. Physical abuse involves severe physical punishment for a child's actions. For example, the parent may lose control and hit the child. The second type of abuse is emotional: the parent says cruel things to the child. For example, the parent may tell the child she's stupid or ugly. Emotional abuse harms as much as physical abuse does. Sexual abuse is the third type. In this case, a relative or family acquaintance forces the child to have sex.

The paragraph above helps us understand the different kinds of child abuse by classifying abusive behaviors into one of three different groups.

TIP:

Get in the habit of reading all of your rough drafts aloud to yourself or to others. Doing so will allow you to hear how your writing will sound to your audience. When you stumble in your reading over a particular passage, mark it as an awkward section that needs further revision.

Reasons

A final method of development involves explaining the reasons something is true or, in the case of an argumentative topic, why something should be true. This first example comes from a student's essay:

Golf is definitely the most difficult sport I have ever played. When I first watched golf on TV, I thought hitting that little white ball looked easy. But when I began to play, I found out just how hard it is. The golf swing requires extreme precision. Altering your swing just slightly can cause the ball to veer many yards off-target. Even the position of your feet can change the ball's direction. Golf also requires the player to know and adhere to many rules. You can be disqualified in a tournament if you break them.

The writer gives two reasons (the difficulty of mastering the swing and the stringent rules) to explain his idea that golf is challenging.

A second example is from a student's movie review:

I strongly recommend that you see the 1996 film version of William Shakespeare's *Romeo and Juliet*. The dialogue is still Shakespeare's, but the new version updates the story to the 1990s. The characters wield guns instead of swords. Scenes are set against the backdrop of skyscrapers. Characters travel in roadsters and limousines. Everything is adapted to modern times, even though the story is the same. It's still a fascinating tale of forbidden love between two teenagers from feuding families. It stars Leonardo DiCaprio and Claire Danes, two talented actors with chemistry.

This paragraph offers two reasons (the intriguing modern update and the film's two stars) for the movie's success.

A final example comes from a magazine article:

Pet foods can be stored in lidded storage tubs, lidded trash cans, or other similar, large capacity containers. Keeping pet food in a closed container makes sense for a number of reasons: keeping dry foods, such as kibble, moisture free will maintain its texture and taste; you won't be encouraging mice or other sneak-thieves to chew into paper bags or to climb into uncovered containers; and there's less likelihood of your pet sneaking food during non-mealtimes.[13]

The passage above presents three reasons to support the idea in the topic sentence.

| EXERCISE 5.1 | *Identifying Methods of Development* |

Identify the method(s) of development used in each of the following paragraphs.

Narration   Cause and effect
Description   Division
Exemplification   Classification
Process analysis   Reasons
Comparison and contrast

1. To be a successful student, make use of your free time on campus. Go to the library to read, study, or do homework. Instead of socializing, use your free time to study with your classmates. Discuss your reading and quiz each other, especially before tests. Also, use your free time to see your instructor if you have questions or need extra help.

2. An epileptic seizure damages the body. Brain damage is one effect. During an epileptic seizure, a person does not breathe; therefore, oxygen cannot reach the brain. Without oxygen, the brain loses function and becomes disoriented. A second effect is the breaking of bones, which can snap during severe muscle spasms and jerking. Pulled muscles are another common effect of the violent movement.

3. Doctors prescribe a variety of medications for epileptic patients. Tegretol controls the impulses in the central nervous system. Its side effects include nausea, drowsiness, dizziness, changes in blood pressure, and blurred vision. Dilantin reduces the frequency of epileptic seizures. Its side effects are diarrhea, headache, and yellow skin or eyes. A third medication is Mysoline, which controls grand mal seizures. Some of its side effects are appetite loss, mood swings, sore throat, and decreased sexual libido.

4. The Intellifax 900 offers many useful features. Its paper cassette holds 200 sheets of paper and its LCD display shows up to 48 digits. It contains a 60-station memory, 20 of which are one-touch and 40 of which are speed-dial. It allows you to transfer a fax call from any phone in the office. The Intellifax 615 offers fewer features than Intellifax 900. Its LCD display shows only 16 digits, and its paper cassette holds only 164 sheets. Its memory can contain only 40 stations, 10 one-touch and 30 speed-dial. However, it offers the same call

transfer feature as the Intellifax 900. The Intellifax 1350M includes even more impressive features, such as a 256 KB memory for 90 different stations. It can also reduce or enlarge copies.

5. Tuition began its climb in the '70s, when universities suddenly found themselves confronting a fiscal landscape more hostile than any they had faced in the previous quarter-century. Although I did not know it at the time, in my freshman year, 1972, Penn [State University] was emerging from a fiscal crisis. The stage was set in the '50s, when, awash in the ever rising tsunami of federal spending triggered by Sputnik's assault on the nation's pride, Penn and its peers went on a building-and-hiring binge. A surge of Great Society financial-aid money helped them expand even further. New faculty could be supported with miminal strain because the salaries were largely covered by federal grants. From 1960 to 1970, operating expenditures at Penn quadrupled, a rate of increase 10 times that of inflation. More buildings were constructed, including three high-rise dormitories, and more faculty and administrators were hired. Martin Meyerson, president from 1970 to 1981 and now president emeritus, agrees that his predecessors "probably overextended themselves."[14]

6. Drugs are destroying our young athletes. One example is Tom Smith, a great basketball player for Central College who helped his team win an NCAA national championship while high on cocaine. He became addicted in high school. Smith said his high school basketball coach caught him smoking pot. He was scared, but the coach suspended him for only a few games and claimed that bad grades were the reason. Another time, he was caught smoking with a friend. His coach tried to make him stop doing drugs, but he wasn't scared enough to stop.

7. Be sure the goal is definite, not vague. When you have formulated your goal, write it down. Then double-check that it is what you really want, not something that someone wants for you. My neighbor believes that his 12-year-old tennis-playing daughter has the potential to win at Wimbledon. But that is his goal, not hers. She is interested in chemistry and jewelry-designing and working in a greenhouse, interests she would have to give up to become a tennis champion. It is hard for her to disappoint her father, but I hope she will because you have to own your goal in order to achieve it.[15]

Choosing a Method

Good writers choose their methods consciously. After you've decided on the main idea you'll discuss in a paragraph, take a moment to reflect upon which method (or methods) you'll use to develop it. Making such decisions before you compose usually results in paragraphs that are clearer and more fully explained.

How do you know which method will best develop your idea? The topic sentence will often dictate which method you must use. Certain statements lead the reader to form expectations about what will come next. For example, these topic sentences insist that you proceed with a particular method of development:

You can housetrain your puppy in just three days. [Process]

Prom night was a complete disaster. [Narration]

We must keep the store open on Thanksgiving Day. [Reasons]

This house's floor plan would suit a family of four. [Description]

The manager will divide this project into smaller tasks, then assign separate duties to each department member. [Division]

Five different kinds of students attend this college. [Classification]

College is very different from high school. [Contrast]

Other topic sentences, however, will allow you to select one or more different methods of development. For example:

The Carolina Panthers are the best NFL football team.

To further explain this idea, you could *narrate* highlights of a recent game, give *examples* of a few different games that illustrate your point, give *reasons* why they're the best, *describe* some of the players on the team, or explain *causes* for the team's superiority.

This next topic sentence is also one that could be developed with a variety of different methods:

Music can relieve tension and stress.

The writer could *narrate* a personal experience, explain the physiological *effects* of music on the body, or give *examples* of people she knows who use music for relaxation.

> **TIP:**
>
> *As you learn each essential characteristic of effective writing, study how the books, articles, and other things you read demonstrate these specific qualities.*

Combining the Methods

Often, instead of using only one method of development in a paragraph, you'll use two or more in combination to fully explain your idea.

For example, read this paragraph about famous Western actor John Wayne, which comes from a magazine:

[John] Wayne's control of his body was economical—no motions wasted. This gave a sense of purpose to everything he did. <u>He worked out characteristic stances, gestures, ways of sitting on his horse</u>. He learned to choreograph his fight moves with the creative stuntman Yakima Canutt. In stills from his early pictures, even when the face is fuzzy, one can identify Wayne by his pose, his gait, the tilt of his shoulders, the *contrapposto* lean of his hips. Classical sculptors worked out the counterpoised position to convey the maximum of both tension and relaxation, motion and stillness, in the human body: the taut line of the body is maintained through the hip above one leg, which is straight, while the torso relaxes, deviating from rigid lines. Wayne constantly strikes the pose of Michelangelo's David. Sometimes, with a wider throw of the hips, he becomes Donatello's David. Wayne was very conscious of his effects. Richard Widmark used to laugh when Wayne, directing "The Alamo," shouted at his actors, "Goddammit, be *graceful*—like me!"[16]

This paragraph develops the topic sentence with both description and comparison: it provides specific details to help us picture John Wayne's stance, and it also compares him to two famous sculptures to assist us further in forming a mental image of him.

This next example from a student's report uses classification and process analysis:

Builders can choose from two types of concrete. Pretensioned concrete contains embedded steel cables in the lower portion of the beam. These cables are positioned in forms and then stretched by heavy jacks. Concrete is poured into the forms and, when it dries, the jacks are released, putting the concrete in compression. Post-tensioned concrete threads the cables through hollow tubes inside the forms. The concrete is then poured into the forms and, when it dries, the cables are stretched by jacks and wedged against steel plates at the ends of the beam.

This writer discusses the two types of concrete, including a step-by-step explanation of how each is made.

Another student's report includes a paragraph that develops the main idea with classification and reasons:

<u>We evaluated four types of parking spaces for the new lot</u>. Spaces can be angled at 30, 45, 60, or 90 degrees. The design team researched actual parking areas and recommends the 45-degree angle. This permits the maximum aisle width. Also, this angle allows drivers easy access, creates less confusion, and supports the traffic pattern we selected.

Not only does the student categorize parking into four different types, but he also offers the four reasons why one is superior to the others.

This next example, also from a student's report on using lasers to harden surfaces, employs both description and contrast:

Tungsten absorbs more than 96 percent of infrared radiation. A laser beam transforms the coating into columns of wavelengths that trap infrared energy. Another coating called cupric oxide demonstrates similar absorptivity. The cupric oxide coating transforms into a random spread of 1/4-inch wavelengths. Cupric oxide melts at a higher temperature and conducts better, but the metal processing industry still favors a third type, the widely available phosphate coating, which is less expensive.

This passage gives descriptive details to help the reader visualize the appearances of three different types of coatings (tungsten, cupric oxide, and phosphate) and also describes the differences between them.

Another example from a magazine article uses both process analysis and effects:

If we're to revive a sense of responsibility in our children, we must start early. I suggest that working parents save up as much energy as possible for coming home. When you walk in the door, expect the kids to fall apart—they all do. Then gather them up in your arms and cuddle together on the sofa. Once you've all moaned or cheered about the kind of day you had, take them into the kitchen with you and let them help you prepare dinner. Later on, they can help with the cleanup. They also should have some regular chores that contribute to the running of the household. Giving them an important role lets them be part of the give and take of a family, instead of just the take. It also allows them to have the joy of experiencing their own effectiveness.[17]

This paragraph not only gives instructions we can follow, but also concludes with an explanation of the benefits (results) of following this procedure.

This next example develops the main idea with a process analysis and one example:

To move forward, you must be convinced that the trip is worth it, that the benefits of making a change exceed the sacrifices. Try weighing the pros and cons. Write a list of gains you can expect, especially immediate benefits, not just long-term ones. List personal, specific reasons to change, says Edwin Fisher, Ph.D., director of the Center of Health Behavior Research at Washington University. While stress management has numerous benefits, it may become meaningful only when you realize, "It's time I come home from work in a good mood for my children."[18]

After explaining the steps in making a change, the writer offers, in the last sentence, an example of changing the way you handle stress.

Another magazine article uses both causes and examples:

<u>In his research, Dr. Klinger has found that most daydreams are sparked by things we see, smell, hear, taste or feel, or by an experience that reminds us of our current concerns.</u> Watching an argument in a movie, for example, might trigger a brief reverie about a conflict with a co-worker and help you see it in a new light that provides a possible solution. Reading a book in which two friends rendezvous for lunch might spark a vignette about running into an old college buddy, which reminds you to call and invite her to dinner. In other instances, the mind stages its own theatrical productions, drawing from its own storehouse of memories and knowledge.[19]

This passage discusses the causes of daydreams and then adds some specific examples for illustration.

Finally, this passage from a book combines classification with examples:

In science, analytical thinking is involved in, say, comparing one theory of dreaming to another; creative thinking is involved in formulating a theory or designing an experiment; practical thinking is involved in applying scientific principles to everyday life. In literature, analytical thinking is involved in analyzing plots, themes, or characters; creative thinking in writing a poem or a short story; practical thinking in applying lessons learned from literature to everyday life. In history, analytical thinking is involved in thinking about how two countries or cultures are similar and different; creative thinking in placing oneself in the position of other people from other times and places; practical thinking in applying the lessons of history to the present. In art, analytical thinking is involved in analyzing an artist's style or message;

creative thinking in producing art; practical thinking in deciding what will sell, and why, in the art world. Even in sports, all three kinds of thinking are needed: analytical thinking in analyzing an opponent's strategy, creative thinking in coming up with one's own strategy, and practical thinking in psyching out the opponent.[20]

This author not only classifies thinking into three different types (analytical, creative, and practical), but offers examples of each in different fields of endeavor (science, literature, history, art, and sports).

EXERCISE 5.2   *Choosing Methods of Development*

Which method(s) of development can be used to develop each of the following topic sentences?

Narration	Cause and effect
Description	Division
Exemplification	Classification
Process analysis	Reasons
Comparison and contrast	

1. Parents should make their children wear bicycle helmets to prevent injury.

2. Raising the minimum wage will save the government millions of dollars.

3. People join cults for different reasons.

4. The audience learns a lot about Othello's pagan background from the characters' conversations in the first act of the play.

5. For many, being a single parent means dealing with financial problems.

6. Children's television programs have changed radically over the last twenty years.

7. Some sexually transmitted diseases permanently damage the reproductive system.

8. Most of the major characters in William Faulkner's fiction come from one of three social groups: the upper-class Southern aristocrats, the poorer country people, and the Negroes.

9. All of these manufacturers offer similar warranties to cover repair costs.

10. Last Saturday night, the emergency room was especially hectic.

11. A dog is particularly well-suited to detect the scent of a human.

12. Honey is sold in four ways: as liquid honey, comb honey, chunk style, or creamed honey.[21]

13. Making good iced tea is simple.

Transitions

Chapter 4 of this book mentioned that clue words help the reader understand the relationships between sentences and thus enable her to better follow the writer's train of thought. Transitions are one type of clue word. Together with clear methods of development, they provide coherence to paragraphs.

Different kinds of transition words indicate different kinds of relationships between ideas.

Narration		*Description*	
before	then	above	on top
during	meanwhile	below	inside
after	later	to the left	outside
next	while	to the right	in front
last		under	in back
		beneath	next to
		over	

Exemplification	*Process*
for example	first, second, third
for instance	next
	then
	after

Comparison

similarly
in like manner
likewise

Cause and Effect

as a result
thus
so
therefore
consequently
because

Reasons

first, second, third
finally
last
furthermore
also

Contrast

on the other hand
however
conversely
in contrast
but
yet
whereas
although
on the contrary

Classification

one, two, three, etc.
first, second, third, etc.

Use transition words in your paragraphs to help the reader easily understand the relationships between your sentences.

TIP:

For more about transition words, see page 80.

EXERCISE 5.3 *Transitions*

Add transitions to the following paragraphs to improve their coherence. (Hint: Identify the method(s) of development first, then add appropriate transitions from the lists in this chapter.)

1. Computer users will appreciate the improvements included in Windows 98. It works faster and more efficiently. It takes less time to open and close programs. The thorough on-line help system has been improved to make it easier to find answers to your questions.

Windows 98 makes connecting hardware to your computer easier. The file allocation table has been improved to save more space on your hard drive.

2. The most common side effect of hepatitis B vaccination is soreness where the shot is given. Tenderness at the injection site has been reported in up to 46% of infants vaccinated. Of children who get the vaccine, 2% to 5% may get a fever greater than 102 degrees Farenheit or become irritable. When hepatitis B vaccine is given with other childhood vaccines, it does not make these mild reactions worse than would be seen with the other vaccines alone. HBIG has sometimes been associated with swelling and hives. As with any drug, there is a slight chance of allergic or more serious reactions with either the vaccine or HBIG. No serious reactions have been shown to occur due to the hepatitis B recombinant vaccines.[22]

3. [Olive oil and corn oil] contain the same number of calories (all of them from fat) and neither contains cholesterol. Their fat type differs dramatically. Olive oil contains mostly cholesterol-lowering monounsaturated fat and a small amount of polyunsaturated fat, otherwise known as linoleic acid. Linoleic acid is essential for good health, though you need only about a teaspoon daily. Corn oil contains very little monounsaturated fat. It's loaded with linoleic acid—probably more than you need. Research tells us that a diet rich in linoleic acid may lower cholesterol levels (which is good). It seems to lower "good" HDL cholesterol levels in the process (which is bad).[23]

4. To form a corporation in North Carolina, complete an application containing the articles of incorporation and file it with the secretary of state. The articles become the corporation's charter, authorizing it to do business. Stockholders who have invested in and formed the corporation must meet to elect a board of directors and establish bylaws to direct the company's activities. The board of directors appoints the corporate officers.

Chapter Summary

We achieve coherence in our paragraphs in two ways. First, we explain our ideas using recognizable **methods of development.** These methods include **narration, description, exemplification, process analysis, comparison and contrast, cause and effect, division, classification,** and **reasons.** Often, we can **combine two or more methods** to more adequately explain an idea. Some topic sentences dictate which method must be used; others allow the writer to select from a variety of appropriate choices. The second way to achieve coherence is by including **transitions** to help the reader understand the relationship between the sentences.

Suggested Writing Activities

As you write one or more of the following compositions, consciously choose appropriate methods of development and transitions:

1. Argue that a particular restaurant is the best one in your town.

2. Think of a product or service you need, then write a report comparing three different brands or providers.

3. Write an essay about dieting.

4. Write a letter of advice about being a successful student.

5. Write a report about one of the following topics: recycling, poetry, labor unions, low-fat cooking, the Internal Revenue Service, the Internet, or cigarettes.

6. Write a report about a small business you'd like to start. Include descriptions of your product or service, your potential customers, your competition, and equipment you'd need.

Notes

1. Robert J. Sternberg, *Successful Intelligence* (New York: Simon and Schuster, 1996), 142.

2. Mark Hosenball and Russell Watson, "Fly the Risky Skies," *Newsweek* (August 18, 1997), 42.

3. The Lakeside Collection, Inc., *The Gifts of Christmas 1997* (Skokie, Ill., 1997), 193.

4. Jo Caudert, "How to Be a Winner," *Woman's Day* (August 5, 1997), 79.

5. Sternberg, 142.

6. Susan Chollar, "Boost Your Energy," *Woman's Day* (July 15, 1997), 76.

7. "Breakthroughs," *Discover* (July 1996), 28.

8. Lea Beazley, "Woodpeckers Live in Most State Parks," *The News Herald*, Morganton, N.C. (July 17, 1997), 4A.

9. George F. Will, "Alomar in Context," *Newsweek* (April 14, 1997), 88.

10. Sternberg, 23.

11. C. Hugh Holman and William Harmon, *A Handbook to Literature* (New York: Macmillan, 1992), 401.

12. Debbie Goldberg, "How to Nurture Your Child's Learning Style," *Family Circle* (September 1, 1997), 80. Reprinted by permission of the author.

13. Betsy Model, "Shopping Big," *Mother Earth News* (August/ September 1997), 46.

14. Erik Larson, "Why Colleges Cost Too Much," *Time* (March 17, 1997), 48. Copyright © 1997 Time, Inc. Reprinted by permission.

15. Caudert, 78.

16. Garry Wills, "John Wayne's Body," *The New Yorker* (August 19, 1996), 44.

17. T. Berry Brazelton, M.D., "Values That Make a Family Strong," *Family Circle* (July 15, 1997), 39.

18. Nick Gallo, "Challenge to Change," *Better Homes and Gardens* (January 1997), 46.

19. Stacey Colino, "Your Most Powerful Creative Force," *Family Circle* (September 1, 1997), 44.

20. Sternberg, 149.

21. Nancy King Quaintance, "The Buzz About Honey," *Our State* (August 1997), 14.

22. U.S. Department of Health and Human Services, Centers for Disease Control, "Hepatitis B" (May 27, 1992).

23. Liz Applegate, Ph.D., "Food Face-Off," *Runner's World* (September 1997), 26.

SIX

Cohesive Paragraphs

Within a long composition, we must divide our ideas into smaller, logical units to help the reader not only to follow our train of thought, but also to see the relationships among different ideas. These smaller, logical units of thoughts are our paragraphs. Each unit of thought should present only one main idea to the reader, along with a complete explanation of that idea. A **cohesive paragraph,** one that "sticks together," is one that discusses only one idea. All of the sentences in the paragraph stick together to support that one point.

When a writer tosses too many different ideas into one unit, two problems result. First, she forces the reader to sort them out, which is a frustrating and confusing task. Second, the writer probably isn't fully explaining each separate idea with adequate layers of development, which are discussed in Chapter 4. For example, read the following paragraph from a magazine:

Shrimp is certainly one of the more popular North Carolina seafoods, as evidenced by the fact that more than 5.2 million pounds are landed annually by commercial fishermen in our state. Shrimp are actually crustaceans of the *Decopoda* type, meaning they have ten legs. They range in size and are graded and priced by the number per pound. As is expected, the larger the shrimp, the higher the price. According to

Jess Hawkins of the North Carolina Division of Marine Fisheries, the shrimp harvest usually begins in March or April when the water begins to warm up. He says, "The harvesting starts when the shrimp begin to move around, and crops, depending on the season, can continue through December."[1]

This paragraph actually contains four different main ideas:

1. The popularity of shrimp
2. A description of shrimp
3. The worth of shrimp in the seafood market
4. The length of the shrimp harvest

Each of the above ideas should be developed in a separate paragraph. But, because they are all thrown together into one paragraph, none of them is adequately explained. To further develop the idea about the popularity of shrimp, the writer should offer additional evidence besides the number caught each year. For instance, she could mention the number of North Carolinians who say shrimp is their favorite seafood, and she could state the percentage of dishes on restaurant menus that include shrimp as an ingredient. To further develop the next idea (shrimp's physical characteristics), she should provide more descriptive details about the shrimp's appearance. For the third idea, she should provide more specific data about size ranges and give current prices for different sizes. The last idea about the shrimp harvest should be further explained by giving more information about how this harvesting is accomplished. Do fishermen use nets or traps? Where do shrimp harvests occur? Because all of these different ideas have been lumped together in one brief paragraph, the reader does not get enough information to fully understand any of them.

Another example of a noncohesive paragraph comes from a leaflet about vaccinations:

There are some differences among the [*Haemophilus* b] vaccines. However, all of the vaccines are considered to be effective. Not all of the vaccines are approved for use in infants. The *Haemophilus* b conjugate vaccine is given by injection. More than 90 percent of infants respond to 2–3 doses of the vaccines approved for infants by making substances in their blood (antibodies) that provide long-term protection against the severe diseases caused by *Haemophilus* b bacteria.

However, several days are required for any protection to be obtained after immunization. Whether the vaccine provides protection against ear infections caused by *Haemophilus* b bacteria is not known. It does not protect against disease caused by other types of *Haemophilus.* The vaccine does not protect against meningitis caused by other bacteria. The vaccine does not cause *Haemophilus* disease. The *Haemophilus* b conjugate vaccine first became available in 1988 and its use for infants first became recommended in 1990.[2]

This paragraph, like the one about shrimp, includes quite a few different major ideas:

1. Differences between vaccines

2. How the vaccine is administered

3. How the vaccine works

4. Diseases not affected by the vaccine

5. The vaccine's history

Therefore, the paragraph is difficult to follow. Not only does it jump from one idea to another without providing any transitions to help the reader understand relationships between the sentences, it lumps all of these separate ideas into one unit and then fails to adequately explain each one. The paragraph above should be divided into five separate paragraphs. Then, additional layers of development should be added to more fully explain each point.

A writer can produce two types of noncohesive paragraphs. The first results when the writer begins with one idea, and then veers off the subject as he composes, discussing something related but off the original topic. This is a natural and common occurrence, for our brains constantly "free associate"; in other words, one thought leads us instantly to another related thought, which leads to another thought. This is how we think, so if we're not paying attention, we might write this way. For example, examine the following paragraph from a student's essay:

Unemployed immigrants who cannot speak English need education. They can't have a better life in this country without the ability to read and to communicate. The alternative is a life of homelessness and possibly even crime. *Illegal aliens who flee from their homelands should be returned because we just can't let everyone in.*

This writer starts off just fine, presenting the idea that education is critical to immigrants' success and developing it with possible effects of being unable to communicate. However, he forgot his main idea as he composed that last sentence of the paragraph, which introduces a completely new idea, the notion that illegal aliens should not be allowed to enter this country. That's a subject for a separate paragraph.

TIP:

How long should a composition be? The length of a paper is directly related to the scope of the topic and to your purpose in writing about it. Never pad your compositions with unnecessary information or extra words to lengthen them.

It's very easy to get sidetracked as we write, to go off on tangents when related ideas pop into our minds. Unfortunately, while writing this way makes perfect sense to the writer who's doing the thinking, the reader will find it difficult to follow. Therefore, a writer must pay attention as she composes, making sure that each of her paragraphs sticks to one main idea. The following paragraph, which comes from a student's research paper advocating school uniforms, provides a good illustration of how this happens:

Peer pressure strongly influences children. School uniforms can reduce a child's fear of becoming a social outcast because of his clothing. "The initial idea," says attorney Nate Bush, "is to get rid of the social stigma attached to not having the right sneakers or jeans." Uniforms prevent social exclusion based on superficial factors such as appearance, and gangs can no longer display their colors. Students who all dress alike experience more of a sense of unity among themselves. As a result, schools in Baltimore, Long Beach, Los Angeles, and San Diego now require their elementary and middle school students to wear matching uniforms. *Mary Hatwood Futrell, former executive director of the National Education Association, said that "the uniform programs that are being instituted in some public schools are an effort to eliminate some of the dangers some students face when wearing expensive clothing. It can provide an element of safety." Schools that require uniforms are often safer and don't need metal detectors, which violate students' constitutional rights.*

The writer begins this paragraph focusing on one specific effect of wearing uniforms, the elimination of peer pressure and social stigma. However, he gets sidetracked into a discussion of a different effect, the increased safety of wearing uniforms. This leads to another digression in the final sentence, which mentions the problem with metal detectors. The loss of cohesion began in the fifth sentence, when the writer brings up the idea of gangs to develop his point about how clothing can be used to divide and pit children against one another. This point about gangs led him naturally to reflect on the potential dangers of clothing, so he focuses on this idea for the rest of the paragraph. The result: a paragraph that strays from its original intentions, one that ends up discussing too many different ideas.

Admittedly, the writer of this paragraph *could* present all of these ideas in one unit if he could more clearly explain the cause and effect relationship between them (see Chapter 5 about using methods of development). But as it stands now, the paragraph promises the reader a discussion of how uniforms could wipe out peer pressure and social stigma; therefore, the writer should stick to that one idea and save the other ideas for other paragraphs.

This next paragraph from a student's literary analysis essay offers another example of a digression from the main idea. The section that violates the paragraph's cohesion is italicized:

African Americans have a rich tradition of expressing themselves through music. Langston Hughes refers to this tendency in the fourth stanza of his poem when he points out that slaves sang sad songs about the cruelty, labor, and injustice they faced. Singing helped them preserve their sanity during back-breaking work in the cotton fields. The speaker in Hughes's poem carried his sorrowful songs "all the way from Africa to Georgia," a reference to the misery of being abducted from Africa and then forced to work for nothing. *Even after slavery was abolished, the mistreatment did not end. That's when the songs changed from "slave songs" to ragtime. Ragtime is related to the blues, which black people knew well. White people also enjoyed ragtime, and some whites even tried to copy it by impersonating a black person, which was called being in "black face."*

In the paragraph above, the writer forgets that she is discussing how Langston Hughes's poem reflects the songs of slaves, and ends up telling us about the historical developments in black music.

TIP:

For more information about organizing ideas effectively, see Chapter 7.

A second type of noncohesive paragraph results when the writer is not sure before or during composing what single idea she wants to discuss in the paragraph. This uncertainty produces a paragraph that rambles from one idea to another. For example, read the following paragraph, which comes from a newsletter about recycling:

The numbers that appear on the bottoms of plastic containers combined with the container types help identify those that local recycling programs will pick up. For example, many towns will not pick up *all* detergent bottles, but they will pick up #2HDPE detergent bottles because they're in high demand for recycling. *Some of the most typical recycled containers are: #1 soda and juice bottles, #2 milk jugs and detergent bottles. You only need to rinse bottles lightly with cold water to prevent bug infestation and spoilage while they are in storage before recycling.*[3]

This paragraph discusses all of the following related but different ideas:

1. Types of containers that recycling programs will pick up
2. Two types of recyclable containers
3. Procedures for cleaning and storing recyclables

The lack of a clear topic sentence causes this paragraph's lack of cohesiveness. If the writer had written one clear statement that identified his main point, he could have stuck to that one focus, rather than including so many different points.

For another example, examine this paragraph from a student's literary analysis:

Chaucer's writing creates verisimilitude, the appearance of truth. His characters are fictional, but they are very much like real people we've known. For example, the Pardoner, who is supposed to be holy and pious, sells fake relics for his own profit. Most of us can recall at least one modern religious man who preaches about morals on Sunday and then participates in schemes to pad his own pockets. The Pardoner is a hypocrite who makes money by exploiting Christians. *The love of money is the root of evil, which is still true today. Money destroys people by nurturing greed.*

This paragraph starts off clearly, developing the idea that readers recognize Chaucer's characters by providing a good example from one of his tales. But then the writer forgets her focus, rambling on to offer a few ideas about the corrupting power of money.

Another noncohesive paragraph comes from a magazine article:

[Lewis] Carroll enthusiast Edward Wakling says: "*Alice [in Wonderland] is clearly the work of a mathematician.*" Quizzes abound, e.g. the White Queen's quiz: "Divide a loaf by a knife—what's the answer to that?" *Laws of nature are repealed: a cake is handed around first and sliced up afterwards; to approach the Red Queen, you walk away from her.* Wonderland *plays off cards, and* Looking-Glass *plays on a chess board. Witty inversions are everywhere. Scholar Martin Gardner says that Dodgson [Lewis Carroll's real name] "seemed to function best when he was seeing things upside down,"—he often amused children by playing music boxes backwards, and children would receive letters from the famous author beginning, "CLD, Uncle loving your" and ending "Nelly dear my," or letters written backwards needing the reflection of a mirror to read them. The Cheshire cat vanishes from its tail end to its disconcerting grin—did it originate from a popular Cheshire product of the time, cheeses molded in the shape of a cat, and perhaps eaten this way? To "grin like a Cheshire cat" was a common expression in Dodgson's day.*[4]

This passage starts out by focusing on how Lewis Carroll's writing exhibits his interest in mathematics, but by the third sentence, the writer is off to another idea: the inversions in Carroll's writing and letters. Then the paragraph takes another detour at the end when the writer turns to a discussion of the origins of one of Carroll's characters, the Cheshire cat.

One final example is from a student's research paper:

Child molestation is difficult to punish because the judicial system works against the child. *Before January 1, 1995, child molestation was a Class H felony punishable by a ten-year prison sentence, or a fine, or both. After January 1, 1995, child molestation became a Class F felony punishable by a twenty-year sentence, a fine, or both. Child molestation ends the victim's childhood. His memories of being molested will plague him his whole life.*

This writer was not sure of his focus before he began; that's why he rambles from the difficulty of enforcement to a history of the penalties to the effects of molestation on the child.

TIP:

> *If you're struggling with every single sentence and the right words just won't come to you, walk away from the composition. Let your subconscious mind work on the paper for a while, then try to write again later.*

How can you make sure your paragraphs are cohesive? Do several things during the planning, writing, and rewriting stages:

Planning

1. Use invention strategies to get ideas. Decide on the one main idea you wish to discuss. Refer back to Chapter 1.

2. Organize your ideas for the *whole* composition before you begin to write. Plan the order in which you'll discuss them. Chapter 7 presents a detailed discussion of this procedure.

Composing

3. For each paragraph, write a topic sentence that clearly states the main idea. This sentence will help you focus on one idea at a time.

4. Refer back to your topic sentence as you write each developing sentence to make sure you're sticking to that one idea.

5. Use method(s) of development (which are discussed in Chapter 5).

Revising

6. Re-evaluate each paragraph after you've completed the entire composition. Be willing to reorganize, to remove sentences that belong elsewhere, or to divide one paragraph into two smaller paragraphs, adding more layers of development if necessary.

7. Examine the length of your paragraphs. Very long paragraphs may not be cohesive. Check them carefully for digressions or too many main ideas.

EXERCISE 6.1   *Cohesive Paragraphs*

Identify the sentence or sentences that prevent the following paragraphs from being cohesive:

1. Handicapped individuals, too, deserve community services. They deserve housing, health care, training and education, employment, and transportation. An individual should be able to move freely about the community, and we should encourage him to do so. Some group home directors are reluctant to let residents leave because they fear accidents and public ridicule.

2. The guitar is easy to play. In just a few days, I learned simple songs such as "Jingle Bells." In just a few weeks, I learned more complicated chords. Now I can play all of my favorites. I love the time I spend practicing my guitar every day. It relieves stress and gives me a creative outlet.

3. Follow-the-leader is the Jazzercise technique. Each 55-minute to 60-minute class is comprised of routines choreographed by Judi to the latest popular songs. New routines are videotaped at eight-week intervals and shipped to instructors worldwide. The program is non-competitive and designed to suit all fitness levels. Instructors are certified through an intensive workshop covering exercise physiology, human anatomy, and dance technique. They are also trained to cue

participants on exercise modifications, pacing, correct breathing, and other safety tips. Ongoing training includes regular monitoring in class, annual CPR certification, regional meetings and conventions and a constant flow of educational materials from the corporate headquarters.[5]

4. Many people oppose the death penalty. They argue that many murders happen due to sudden emotional impulse, such as an angry husband who kills his wife. A person who acts out his emotions can't make a rational decision, and he can't understand the severity of the punishment that awaits him. The death penalty, therefore, would not deter this type of criminal. A person must remember that capital punishment could cause the death of innocent people. Many don't care about that possibility as long as the death penalty deters crime. One must consider the negative and positive effects and determine which are greater. If we can reduce murder rates through capital punishment, we should continue to use it frequently to warn would-be criminals. To me, the positive outweighs the negative. Capital punishment is effective when used often with plenty of media coverage.

Chapter Summary

Cohesive paragraphs help the reader follow our ideas. Make sure each of your paragraphs presents and develops only *one* main idea. Don't mix several different ideas in the same paragraph or stray from your first idea.

Suggested Writing Activities

As you write one or more of the following compositions, evaluate each paragraph for cohesiveness:

1. Describe a specific disease affecting yourself, a relative, or a friend.
2. Write an essay about going on blind dates.

3. Write a review of a book you've read.

4. Write a report about a nonprofit organization you support.

5. Write a memo to a co-worker to propose a change in a procedure at your workplace.

Notes

1. Nancy King Quaintance, "Flavors from the Sea," *Our State* (July 1997), 15.

2. Department of Environment, Health, and Natural Resources, Immunization Branch, Centers for Disease Control, "Important Information About *Haemophilus* Influenzae Type b Disease and *Haemophilus* b Conjugate Vaccine" (1991).

3. Robert Lilienfeld, *The ULS Report Newsletter* (Ann Arbor, Mich.), quoted in Janet Sobesky, "Ask the Experts," *Woman's Day* (July 18, 1995), 25.

4. Mary Hutchison, "Lewis Carroll," *Britannia* (September 1995), 8.

5. Jazzercise, Inc., Carlsbad, Calif., "Jazzercise News Release."

SEVEN

Organizing Logical Units

*W*riting can be compared to collecting butterflies. Writers have a lot of thoughts and ideas, which are the "butterflies" flitting about in our minds. These "butterfly" ideas come in a variety of types: some are large, some are small, some are blue, some are yellow, some are black, some are orange. Some are spotted, some are striped, some are solid. But they all fly together around in our heads, tumbling in and over each other, weaving in and out of our consciousness. When we compose, we seek to offer the reader an understanding of what some of these "butterflies" in our minds are like.

Before we can do that, though, we must find a way to arrange them so that we can describe them logically to someone who can't see them. We must find a way to organize them before we present them to a reader. We might think of this organizing process as "netting" the butterflies and placing them into "jars" according to characteristics they share. For instance, we could place all of the blue butterflies in one jar. Or we could put all of the large butterflies in a jar. Or we could group all of the striped ones together. This helps the person examining our collection understand the butterflies better.

Prior to letting a reader examine our collection of ideas, we must determine the most logical way to group them. One expert on thinking says that "much of what we call 'intelligence' is our ability to recognize patterns."[1] Intelligent writing, therefore, is organized according to discernible patterns. When we prepare to write, we determine these patterns by finding logical categories for organizing ideas. Doing so will help our reader better understand what we want to say.

Organizing things into categories is a task we're all familiar with. The clothes in your dresser drawers, for instance, are probably divided into different categories. You might place socks in one drawer, underclothes in another, and shirts in another. In this case, the category you use to separate these articles of clothing is *type of clothes*. You store different types in different drawers, rather than jumbling them all together.

However, when it's time to do laundry, we reorganize those clothes using a different category: *color*. Now you separate those same clothes into piles you label whites, pastels, and colors.

You may have categorized other things in your home as well. The food in your kitchen might be organized according to *type of food* (different cabinets for canned goods, spices, and cereals). The homework you need to complete could be separated according to *subject* (different notebooks or folders for English, math, and biology). The bills you need to pay might be arranged according to *due dates* (electric bill and phone bill this Friday, rent and car payment next Friday, etc.).

Just as you find categories for things to help you understand and manage them better, you must find categories for your ideas that will help your reader comprehend them. When you present your thoughts in logical units, the reader can more easily grasp your meaning. This means that a writer must spend some time determining the best organization plan for his entire composition *before* he begins to write. After determining what he'd like to say, he must next decide on the categories he'll use to arrange how he'll say it.

When a writer skips this important step and begins to write without planning ahead, his composition will often ramble or jump from thought to thought. At best, the reader of such a composition will experience difficulty accessing specific information. At worst, the reader will fail to understand the writer's ideas and feel confused or frustrated. For example, read the following passage from a newsletter:

Once again, the Ashe County Runners Club will be hosting the longest running adult biathlon and five-kilometer road race in this area. The race, now in its ninth year, has become a tradition.

The race has seen several national champions compete over the years. Though it's early to know who may sign up for this year's event, you can expect some determined competition in several of the age categories.

The biathlon was created in 1991 by local runners and bicycle enthusiasts, who started the race to give area athletes an annual challenge. The lively competitive atmosphere and camaraderie help many runners create life-long friendships as well. Steve Wilson directed the race for seven years. In 1998, he turned the race over to Misty Holland. The Club maps out various courses for the race from year to year, but all of them take runners around the Crystal Lake area.

This year, the races will be returning to the Crystal Lake area, to be hosted by the Ashe County Runners Club and directed by Misty Holland. On May 2 at 8:00 A.M., the ninth running of the event will take place. The 5K race will start in the parking lot of Kennedy High School. The biathlon race will start at 8:15 A.M. and will begin in the parking lot as well.

Powerful competitors such as college-level cross-county runners, representatives from the military, and local biathletes and triathletes are expected to attend. The race will also include a children's class for anyone under twelve years of age.

The bike race in particular is exciting to watch. Spectators are welcome, with the best viewing area being the hill on Waterview Road.

This writer did not organize her thoughts before composing; instead, she just wrote down details in the order in which she thought of them. As a result, the article jumps around in a confusing manner. A list of topics discussed in each paragraph makes this clear:

PARAGRAPH 1:   Sponsor of race

History of race

PARAGRAPH 2:   History of race

Competitors

PARAGRAPH 3:   History of race

Benefits of participating

Sponsor/organizer of race

Where the race will take place

PARAGRAPH 4:   When and where the race will take place

Sponsor/organizer of race

PARAGRAPH 5:   Competitors

PARAGRAPH 6:   Where to watch the race

However, because the author did not determine her categories before beginning to write, the information is all mixed up. For instance, she discusses the race's history in paragraphs 1, 2, and 3, mixing these details with other types of information. She discusses competitors in paragraph 2, and then brings up that same topic again in the fifth paragraph. The what, when, and where details are sprinkled throughout. As a result, the information is difficult to follow.

To improve this article, the writer should sort the details into the four categories listed above. But even then, she's still not ready to compose. The next step involves determining the most logical order for these categories. Should she present the details of the race first, then move to a discussion of competitors and the race's history? Or should she present the race's history first, leading to her information about when and where the race will take place? Again, the writer must select an order that seems most logical, one that will make the most sense to the reader.

Another example of a composition that lacks logical organization is a letter to a newspaper editor:

On Friday, May 23, my family's guinea pig got out of his cage. He disappeared from our home on Oak Drive.

My father was in the hospital at the time. My mom put his cage on the back porch, which she always did to give him some fresh air. I am their son. I bought the guinea pig when he was a baby.

We hand-fed him until he would eat by himself. My father became very attached to the guinea pig. We had a cat, but she was killed by a car. We had that cat for twelve years.

Frank the Guinea Pig was a great companion for my father. When I got home on the day Frank disappeared, my mother was crying when she told me the guinea pig had escaped from his cage. I went to see my father that day in the hospital.

I had to tell him that Frank was gone, and my father was devastated. We're hoping that someone has seen him. He means so much to us, and we love him and miss him. If anyone has any information about our guinea pig, please contact us.

Listing the topics in each paragraph reveals the organizational problems:

PARAGRAPH 1:   The day the guinea pig disappeared

PARAGRAPH 2:   The day the guinea pig disappeared

How they acquired the guinea pig

PARAGRAPH 3:   The guinea pig's upbringing

Their feelings for the guinea pig

Their pet cat

PARAGRAPH 4:   Their feelings for the guinea pig

The day the guinea pig disappeared

PARAGRAPH 5:   Their feelings for the guinea pig

Again, clear categories emerge when we examine the information included in this letter:

What happened the day the guinea pig disappeared

The guinea pig's history with the family

Their feelings for the guinea pig

To improve the reader's understanding of this information, the details need to be sorted into the three categories listed above, and then the letter should be rewritten to include three logical paragraphs, one for each category of information.

Now that we've established the importance of grouping like information together, let's look next at how to discover and arrange the best categories for our ideas.

TIP:

For more information about writing a paragraph that discusses only one main idea, see Chapter 6.

The Thesis Statement

Before you can decide on the most logical categories for your ideas, you'll need to determine what you'd like to say. What one major idea or concept would you like the reader to know or to believe by the time he has completed reading your letter, your essay, your memo, or your report? The answer to this question becomes your **thesis statement.** For example, your thesis in a letter to your gas company might be:

My last monthly statement contains an error that needs to be corrected.

Your thesis in your report on characteristics of the Democratic political party might be:

Democrats believe in strong presidential leadership, civil rights, and programs that benefit middle-class workers.

Your thesis in your memo to those you supervise might be:

Every employee must wash his or her hands thoroughly after clocking in.

The thesis statement, which should always be clearly stated near the beginning of your composition, announces your main point. An effective thesis statement possesses the following three characteristics:

1. **It is stated in one declarative sentence.** This is the *one* point you want your reader to remember, so write one clear, succinct sentence to state that point.
2. **It is stated assertively.** Omit phrases such as *I think that* or *I believe that* and just state the idea.
3. **It is specific.** In anticipation of the rest of your essay, you should include the reasons this idea is true or should be true.

Formulating a clear thesis statement is the first step toward logical organization of your ideas, for you have to know exactly what you're trying to say before you begin trying to say it. As a matter of fact, a good thesis will often suggest the most sensible organization pattern, as we'll see in the next section.

TIP:

For more about writing assertive statements, see Chapter 10.

Discovering Categories for Ideas

Once you have determined your thesis statement, you're ready to decide how to collect and categorize the ideas you want to present. How do you know which categories to choose to logically sort your thoughts? Unfortunately, there is often no right or wrong answer. Each subject might be organized in a variety of different ways.

For example, if you decided to organize your personal collection of videotapes, how would you arrange them? Many people would sort them according to *genre*, grouping tapes together according to their type (drama, comedy, horror, documentary, etc.). But that's not the only way to organize them. You could, instead, group them according to *actors and actresses*. Using that category, you would place all of your Tom Cruise movies in one area, all of your Jack Nicholson tapes in another, and your Angela Bassett movies in another. Or you could arrange them from *most watched to least watched*. You could even organize them according to *length*. The category you chose would depend on your purpose.

When you write, a variety of different categories might be appropriate for arranging your thoughts. Your topic and thesis statement will sometimes dictate which categories you must use. Other topics and thesis statements will require you to apply logic to decide not only what categories you'll use to organize ideas, but also what order you should use to present these categories. In the following sections, thesis statements focusing on different aspects of ballroom dancing will illustrate how a thesis can either dictate certain categories or require you to determine them with your own powers of logical thinking. Using the same subject will demonstrate how your focus (thesis) affects the organization of your thoughts.

Natural Organization

Some subjects organize themselves. If you are recounting a series of events, for example, you will naturally arrange them in chronological order, from the first thing that happened to the last thing that happened. For instance, if your thesis is

The 1997 Ballroom Dance Championship competition was very exciting.

you would probably tell the story of what happened during the various events. Or, if your thesis is

Since childhood, Brad Evans has been training to become a champion ballroom dancer.

you would tell the history of Brad's training. In a report on the history of the tango, your thesis might be

The tango has evolved over the last one hundred years.

To explain this thesis, you would naturally discuss the dance's origins, then its various developments up to modern times.

However, even though narratives organize themselves, you will still need to determine how to divide your longer composition into smaller units. Usually, we relate one incident or describe one scene per paragraph.

Another type of subject that will also organize itself naturally is an explanation of a procedure. Like a narrative, the steps in a process arrange themselves in chronological order, so you present each step in order from the first thing done to the last thing done:

If you can take steps forward, to the side, and backward, you can do the waltz.

However, you will also need to determine how to divide your explanation into smaller units. Usually, we explain each major step in a separate paragraph. The thesis above organizes the composition into three units:

PARAGRAPH 1:   The forward step

PARAGRAPH 2:   The side step

PARAGRAPH 3:   The backward step

Because you would be explaining a procedure, you would naturally discuss the steps in the order they happen.

Other explanations of procedures, however, require a little more logical thought. For instance, read this next thesis:

To effectively lead his partner, the gentleman ballroom dancer must perfect his "frame."

This thesis implies that the writer will offer instructions for improving "frame," which is the way the gentleman holds his arms and upper body. But since frame involves doing several different things simultaneously, a chronological arrangement of the details is not possible. How, then, can the writer organize her information? Applying logic, the writer might decide to organize her advice into units corresponding to each separate body part:

PARAGRAPH 1:   Left arm

PARAGRAPH 2:   Right arm

PARAGRAPH 3:   Torso

PARAGRAPH 4:   Head

In addition to narratives and explanations of procedures, other types of thesis statements will clearly suggest how information can be categorized. For example, a thesis announcing that you'll present reasons suggests you will discuss each separate reason in a separate unit. For example, for the thesis

Older adults should consider enrolling in a ballroom dance class for social, health, and psychological reasons.

the overall organizing category is *reasons*. All that's left for you to do is to determine the most logical order for the presentation of these reasons to the reader. Does it make more sense to arrange them from most important to least important, or vice versa? Or do the reasons themselves suggest a particular order, perhaps because of a cause and effect relationship between them? For example, the thesis above offers three reasons, each of which should be discussed in a separate paragraph. But in what order should you present them? You might want to discuss psychological reasons last, for you could explain how the first two benefits could ultimately lead to the third. Or, you could discuss physical and mental benefits—your most important reasons—first, saving social benefits for last.

Logical Organization

Many of the compositions you'll write will not, unfortunately, organize themselves. Instead, you will have to use logic to determine appropriate categories, as well as the best order for those categories. For example, examine the following thesis statement:

Ladies' ballroom dance costumes are designed to accentuate their movements on the dance floor.

This composition, which focuses on the description of a thing, could be organized using different categories. First of all, you could arrange your details according to the *different parts of the costume*. Your units would then be:

> PARAGRAPH 1:   Dress
>
> PARAGRAPH 2:   Jewelry
>
> PARAGRAPH 3:   Shoes

On the other hand, you could choose a very different category—*materials and methods of construction*—to organize your details. Using this particular category, your plan might be:

> PARAGRAPH 1:   Fabrics (including dress and shoes)

PARAGRAPH 2:   Ornaments (sparkling or shining accessories such as sequins, beads, and jewels worn separately or attached to dress or shoes)

PARAGRAPH 3:   Style (including dress and shoes)

Other thesis statements tend to suggest one particular type of organization plan. For example, for the thesis

International and American styles of ballroom dancing differ in three significant ways.

you would probably organize your composition using *differences* as your category. Your plan then might be:

PARAGRAPH 1:   Costumes

PARAGRAPH 2:   Music

PARAGRAPH 3:   Dance steps

PARAGRAPH 4:   Style

For a report about current champions in the sport, your overall organizing category is obviously *individual champions,* but then you would need to determine categories for your discussion of each separate dancer. Your plan might be:

Champion 1

PARAGRAPH 1:   Training

PARAGRAPH 2:   Technique and style

PARAGRAPH 3:   Accomplishments

Champion 2

PARAGRAPH 4:   Training

PARAGRAPH 5:   Technique and style

PARAGRAPH 6:   Accomplishments

Champion 3

PARAGRAPH 7: Training

PARAGRAPH 8: Technique and style

PARAGRAPH 9: Accomplishments

If your thesis is

In the United States, ballroom dancing is increasing in popularity.

what categories would you use to organize your ideas? You could begin by making a list of all the ways we can see that a sport is becoming more popular:

1. More people participate in it.

2. We see it on television more.

3. It's added to the Olympics or to college athletic programs.

4. Champions of that sport are hired to endorse consumer products in commercials and other advertisements.

5. Formal instruction becomes more widely available.

Some or all of these might become suitable categories for organizing your information. Your overall organizing category is *indicators of a sport's popularity*. In your composition, you might explain your thesis by discussing how ballroom dancing specifically conforms to these signs. As a result, you might plan your units as follows, using each statement as a topic sentence:

PARAGRAPH 1: The opening of new dance studios, along with increasing enrollments at existing studios, indicate that more people want to learn to dance.

PARAGRAPH 2: Media coverage—including televised competitions and commercials that feature dance champions—is increasing.

PARAGRAPH 3: Ballroom dancing is being added to college athletic programs and has received provisional status for inclusion in the Olympic Games.

We've determined three clear units in which to arrange our details. Note how we combined similar information in the initial list (specifically, number 1 with number 5 and number 2 with number 4) to create three different units.

Now let's determine categories for a different thesis:

Many factors are contributing to the rise in popularity of ballroom dance.

Though this thesis is similar to the last one in that both examine the popularity of the sport, it has a different focus. While the first one examined the evidence that reveals the sport's growth, this second thesis focuses on why it's growing; therefore, the resulting composition will be organized according to the category *causes*. To decide on appropriate units, you might again make a list of reasons people get involved in a sport:

1. Physical fitness

2. Fun

3. To socialize and make friends

4. Relaxation

5. Creative innovations in the sport

6. New awareness of the sport

7. Interest in trying something new and different

While you may not want to discuss all of these factors, you could pick out two or three of the ones you feel best account for the growing interest in this particular sport. For example, you might plan your composition as follows:

PARAGRAPH 1: A resurging interest in wholesome fun attracts people to ballroom dance.

PARAGRAPH 2: Increased media coverage is helping people discover this sport for the first time.

PARAGRAPH 3: Creative, interesting innovations in the sport are attracting a younger generation of participants.

Again, notice how we combined information in our initial list to generate three logical units.

TIP:

For more about ways you can discover ideas in a systematic, organized manner, review the left-brain invention strategies discussed in Chapter 1.

EXERCISE 7.1   *Logical Categories*

1. Determine logical categories for organizing the information that will develop each of the following thesis statements:

   a. Robert E. Lee was one of the most skilled generals in military history.

   b. Wolverines are dangerous and solitary animals.

   c. The U.S. Congress should raise the minimum wage.

   d. The White House in Washington, D.C., is a historically and architecturally fascinating structure.

   e. The crime rate is falling due to a number of societal influences.

   f. Anyone can decorate a Christmas tree.

2. Each of the following writing samples is disorganized. Determine the categories of information presented.

   a. My psychology class is only an hour long, but it seems like six hours. The professor lectures the whole time. He does not provide any handouts and only occasionally writes a drawing or chart on the chalkboard. He does not follow the textbook. Therefore, we students are unsure what to focus on when we study. We never do any assignments or exercises to help us understand the material. Sometimes he might ask a few questions about a chapter we read. This professor has taught this subject for twenty years, so he talks over our heads. We don't understand what he is discussing. Then his tests cover stuff he never talked about. He let us take home the first two tests. I looked up every answer and still made only an 85 because he doesn't agree with the book. The answer may be the one found in the text, but he still marks it wrong because it deviates from *his* definition. We took our final test in class, and the average score was only 65. No one knew what to study.

b. A mentally ill person often believes in things that aren't real. Consequently, this creates all kinds of problems. He might become introverted, refusing to speak for fear that others will ridicule him. His pain could turn to anger, which frightens his relatives and friends. People may avoid him, but he needs friendship just like anyone else. A mentally ill person often has no friends. He is often alone, left to think up his own incorrect explanations for why people avoid him. His suffering is caused by his different interpretation of reality. A relative of a mentally ill person should reassure him of his family's love. He needs to be reminded that he is a good person.

c. I have been meaning to read *Cold Mountain* for six months, the length of time it's been on the *New York Times* bestseller list. I found out that there really is a Cold Mountain. It is a 6,000-foot-high mountain about five to six miles southeast of Waynesville, west of Morganton. It is the story of a Confederate soldier in the Civil War who walks away from a terrible war to go back home to his pre-war sweetheart. Frazier is an excellent descriptive writer, and some of his descriptions are of the landscape and of the characters he meets. The book reminded me of two poems about travels, first the *Odyssey*, or the travels of a Greek king, and *Canterbury Tales* by Chaucer, the story of pilgrims journeying from London to Canterbury and the stories they told.[2]

d. The pavilion will measure thirty-six feet by twenty-six feet with a ten-foot ceiling. A two- by three-foot deck will surround it. We'll stack logs for the grill on one side. The inside grill will be built with river rock. Also around the outside of the pavilion, five more grills will be ready for cookouts. Costs vary, so we'll have to check prices just before we begin construction. Also a cabinet will flank both sides of the grill, with a double sink on one side. Picnic tables inside the pavilion measure six feet long and three feet wide. Seven tables will fit inside. On one end of the pavilion we'll build a three-foot stage. One step will lead up to the stage. Hardwood floors will cover the inside. The tables will be made of treated lumber and then stained. The walls will be constructed out of lumber and rock. We'll top it all off with a shingle roof. We'll use wheeled trash cans so we can move them. We'll build four entrances into the pavilion, two with a ramp and two with steps.

Choosing Natural or Logical Organization

Neglecting to determine categories for ideas is one way to ensure organizational problems. Another common way we create organizational problems is by trying to present our ideas using a natural organization pattern when we should determine a logical pattern instead. Specifically, we often inappropriately arrange our thoughts in narrative form. Telling a story is easy and comes naturally, so it's tempting to present our points within a chronological recounting of events. However, this form often buries our ideas in unnecessary details and thus prevents the reader from discerning and understanding them. For example, read the following student essay:

My Career Choice

I worked in retail sales for over twenty years, and I enjoyed it. I liked working with the public, especially in jewelry sales. It was fun, financially rewarding, and socially enriching.

Usually retail salespeople have to work flexible hours, but I worked only Monday through Friday, 9 A.M. to 6 P.M., with weekends off. This was *a great schedule* for me, especially when my children were very young.

But then my employer required all employees to work flexible hours. I had to work some nights and weekends. I made *a lot of money,* and *I liked my co-workers* so I adjusted and stayed.

Then I began wondering what it would be like to work in a different field. I had considered returning to school, but my unpredictable work schedule made that impossible.

Then last February, my employer filed for bankruptcy. I was sad, but at the same time I knew I'd get my chance to get my college degree. So here I am, studying toward my new goal, a degree in paralegal technology.

This writer clearly states her thesis (*it was fun, financially rewarding, and socially enriching*) in her opening paragraph. But then, instead of using the category *reasons I liked retail sales* to organize her information, devoting one unit for explanation of each reason, she relates the story of her history in this career field. As a result, even though she does briefly mention the reasons stated in her thesis (highlighted in italics), this information is mixed in with a lot of irrelevant information that distracts the reader from the essay's main point. This approach also results in insufficient development of the main ideas (see Chapter 4).

Another example comes from a student's essay about pop singer Madonna. At the beginning of his essay, he states this thesis:

Madonna has made a fantastic career out of what little she had through hard work, creativity, and sex appeal.

Though the thesis statement announces specific, clear categories for the writer's information, the paper goes on to use natural organization to present Madonna's chronological life history from her birth to the present. Instead, the writer needs to pick out details from that history to include in each of his categories to help the reader better understand the causes of her success. In this case, a natural organization pattern buries the relevant details in a lot of unnecessary information.

When you choose narrative organization, carefully evaluate whether this is the best method for arranging your ideas. If you're writing a report for your supervisor to explain why a piece of machinery malfunctioned, you might be tempted to tell the story of what happened the day it shut down. However, a better organization pattern for your information might involve considering your details in terms of a category such as *causes for the malfunction* or *defective parts*. If you're writing an essay to analyze a short story, you might initially be tempted to present details in the order they happened in the story. Consider, though, whether you should group these details into categories according to their other similarities, rather than when they occur.

TIP:

When trying to determine the best organization plan for a composition, don't just choose the first pattern you think of. Sketch several possibilities, then evaluate which one will present your information most clearly to the reader.

Outlining

When people express their dislike for outlining, they usually give two reasons they skip this step of the writing process. First, they say, outlining takes too much time. Inexperienced writers figure they can decide on the best order for their ideas as they compose, so why should they spend extra time working that out before writing? Second, they argue that because they don't stick to the original outline and end up changing it to match the finished paper, why bother with one to start with?

Unfortunately, both of these arguments are myths. Outlining is actually a critical step in the composition process, one that should not be omitted for these or any other reasons. An outline is a guideline that improves logical arrangement of the writer's thoughts and prevents rambling or digressing.

Myth 1: Skipping the outlining step saves time.   On the contrary, failing to outline actually adds time to composition. Finding the language to express ideas is difficult enough. When we don't spend time determining a plan of organization before we begin writing, we force our brains to do two challenging mental tasks (organizing and composing) at the same time. Because this is more complicated, the composing is usually slower and often can be more frustrating. Separating the outlining stage and working out the organization of your ideas before you begin to write might actually save you valuable time in the long run, for composition uncomplicated by simultaneous organizing tends to be easier and, therefore, faster.

Myth 2: An outline is useless because the final paper rarely matches it.   A builder never begins constructing a building without a blueprint, or plan, for the finished structure. However, if during construction the builder discovers a better way to do something, he can alter the blueprint to reflect the improvements. Similarly, a writer should not begin a composition without an outline. Creating an outline of your ideas before you write will prevent you from

- digressing from your main point.
- rambling or jumping from thought to thought.

- ◼ mixing different kinds of information.
- ◼ discussing an idea in the wrong place.

The outline is your best determination of the overall structure, but that doesn't mean you won't discover a better way as you're writing. If you do, by all means go with the better plan. An outline is not cast in stone; it's a preliminary guide. Just because you may alter your original plan does not mean that it wasn't useful to help you get started.

Formal Outlines

When most people think of an outline, they picture one that includes Roman numerals. This type uses a combination of Roman-numerals, letters, and Arabic numerals. The following outline, for example, shows a possible plan of organization and development for a thesis statement mentioned earlier:

To effectively lead his partner, the gentleman ballroom dancer must perfect his "frame."

   I. Left arm
      A. Hand
         1. Placement on partner's back
         2. Finger position
      B. Elbow
         1. Position
         2. Firm "lock"

  II. Right arm
      A. Elbow
         1. Position
         2. Firm "lock"
      B. Hand
         1. Grasp of partner's hand
         2. Pressure

III. Torso
      A. Shoulders

    B. Back
    C. Waist
IV. Head position

In this type of outline, the Roman numerals correspond to the major organizing units, while the letters and Arabic numerals list supporting information and examples.

This format is useful for separating ideas and indicating their relationships to each other. It also helps the writer evaluate whether or not he's adequately developing each idea. However, a writer does not necessarily need to use this more rigid form for planning his composition. Instead, he might choose a less formal approach.

Informal Outlines

When a writer is determining the arrangement of a composition, she can sketch ideas in a more informal manner. The point of outlining ahead of composing is to work out the organization of thoughts, so the writer can use any system that provides a useful guideline or map to follow as she composes. Such systems can be as brief as simply making a list of ideas in the order you want to discuss them. Or make a list of topics for each paragraph, as in the previous sections of this chapter. Or use any other approach that makes sense to you. Since this planning is for your eyes only, develop a system that works for you.

One specific informal technique is called *branching*. This involves starting with a topic and then drawing "branches" of subtopics, supporting reasons, main points, cause and effect relationships, examples, and details radiating from that central topic. If you need to write a memo, for instance, to inform your employees of renovations to the building that houses their offices, you could first plan that memo by creating branches of subtopics (reasons, temporary changes, the noise, and permanent changes) you'll need to explain. Then draw more branches from each subtopic branch to outline the specific details you need to present:

TIP:

Always sketch a plan for everything you write, even essay exam questions.

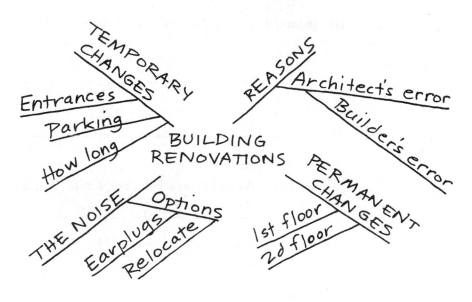

For those writers who like a more visual layout of their ideas, this technique can be a valuable tool for discovering and arranging logical categories.

EXERCISE 7.2   *Outlining*

Fill in the following outline:

Thesis: A homeowner can crime-proof her house several ways.

I. _____

    A. Install deadbolt locks on all outside doors

    B. _____

    C. _____

II. _____

    A. _____

    B. _____

    C. Hire a private security firm to maintain an alarm system.

III. Establish a neighborhood watch program.

    A. _____

    B. _____

    C. _____

IV. _____

    A. _____

    B. Leave the lights on when you go out.

    C. _____

V. _____

    A. Get a dog.

    B. _____

    C. _____

Using Organizational Markers

Organizational markers are different systems for arranging information on the page. They help your reader visually separate ideas and quickly discern their relationships. Using these markers, which include numbers, lists, and headings, helps readers more easily access and understand your thoughts.

For example, the following section from a memorandum presents the writer's suggestions in the form of a list with "bullets" (black dots) that separate the items:

Rules and Regulations

The following are rules for the protection of our park and its visitors:

- The removal of any plant, animal, or rock is prohibited.

- All areas managed by the Division of Parks and Recreation are wildlife preserves. Hunting and trapping are prohibited.

- Firearms and fireworks are not permitted.
- Fires are permitted in designated areas only.
- Camping is permitted in designated areas by permit only.
- The possession or consumption of alcoholic beverages is prohibited.
- Pets must be on a leash no longer than six feet.

Separating each rule from the others using spacing, list format, and bullets improves the document's readability. You can also number the items in the list.

Headings, or minititles for smaller sections of a composition, also help readers separate information and find specific details quickly. An effective heading is a concise but accurate description of the topic discussed in that section. Headings are distinct from the rest of the text; for instance, they might be in bold print, underlined, or in larger letters. One example, which comes from a newspaper article, announces that it will describe "the world of small invertebrates that are living in our streams and lakes"[3] and then labels each section with a bold, large heading that identifies the creature discussed in those particular paragraphs: "Water Pennies," "Clams and Mussels," "Snails," "Dragonflies," and so on. An effective heading system also helps the reader discern the relationships between sections. For example, this book uses large bold type positioned in the margin to label major sections of each chapter, while subsections are italicized and fall within the text body.

Professional writing, such as memorandums and reports, will often include these types of markers to help busy readers find and understand specific pieces of information rapidly.

Chapter Summary

Clear writing is always organized by either a **natural** or **logical** pattern. After determining your **thesis statement,** decide on the best **categories** for grouping your ideas. Before writing, always take the time to create either a **formal** or **informal outline** to guide you as you compose. Finally, consider using **organizational markers** in your composition to help your reader understand and see the relationships among your ideas.

Suggested Writing Activities

Find logical categories and create some type of outline before writing one or more of the following compositions:

1. Write about a challenge you face, *or* your goals, *or* things about yourself you'd like to improve.

2. Write a letter to a former teacher who positively influenced you.

3. Write an essay about your decision to go to college.

4. Write a report comparing different weight loss aids.

5. Write a letter of recommendation for a friend or colleague.

6. Write a brochure that explains a procedure or concept for the customers at your workplace.

Notes

1. Roger von Oech, *A Whack on the Side of the Head* (New York: Warner Books, 1983), 55.

2. Harry L. Wilson, "'Cold Mountain': A Heart-breaking Story of Love, Life, War," *The News Herald,* Morganton, N.C. (January 7, 1998), 4A.

3. Lea Beazley, "Streamlife in Parks Rich and Varied," *The News Herald,* Morganton, N.C. (April 16, 1997), 4A.

EIGHT

Interesting Openings

A good opening paragraph is critical to the success of your composition. First impressions are important because readers often judge your document based on your first few sentences. When a reader can choose whether or not to read the rest of your composition, she usually does so based on what you do (or don't do) in your introductory paragraph. When the reader *must* read your composition, she is likely to decide on its effectiveness (its clarity and its interest) based on those crucial opening statements.

Purposes of the Opening

Whether you're writing a report, a memo, a letter, or any other document, you need to achieve several objectives at the outset. Every effective opening accomplishes four specific tasks:

1. It provides background information.
2. It states your thesis.

3. It establishes the tone of your composition.

4. It stimulates your reader's interest.

To achieve all four objectives, the length of your opening will vary depending on your topic and the scope of the information you plan to include. Openings are at least one paragraph long, but they can be several paragraphs long if, for instance, you'll need to explain a lot of background information.

Give Background Information

The first purpose of the opening is to provide the reader with any necessary background information he needs to understand your topic or idea. The kind of background information you'll include depends on your subject. One type is historical detail that helps the reader understand the past. For example, in an essay advocating the reintroduction of the wolf into certain wilderness areas, you may want to explain the animal's past history in those areas, including why it disappeared. In a report to your supervisor about a committee project, you might want to describe what tasks have already been completed.

Another type of background is a description of the current situation or circumstances of an issue or problem. You might need to give your reader information about what is happening now. For instance, a memo to co-workers about an equipment problem might need to explain the current status of that equipment. A research paper on computer security will probably need to orient the reader with a discussion of concerns confronting computer users today.

Background can also include an explanation of your topic's relevance or importance. Why should the reader be interested in this subject? Why is it meaningful? What are some of its effects? For example, in a paper about the health risks of smoking cigarettes, you might want to establish the prevalence of smoking and smoke exposure. In a letter to your local newspaper editor about the need for a traffic light at a busy intersection, you might want to note how many motorists are affected, as well as how many accidents occur at this location.

A final type of background information is definitions of terminology. You'll want to make sure your reader knows the meaning of significant words to avoid confusion or misinterpretation. For instance, in an essay analyzing a poem, you may want to define specific literary terms you'll be using. In a research paper about the use of the drug Ritalin, you'd want to explain what this drug is, what conditions it treats, and its effects.

State Thesis

Another purpose of the opening paragraph(s) is to state your main idea, or thesis. The thesis is the one sentence that clearly and concisely identifies the one idea you want your reader to know or to believe after reading your paper. Stating your thesis in your opening paragraph focuses the reader's attention on that point.

Where should you state the thesis? In the first sentence of the composition? The last sentence of the introduction? Some place in between? There is no one answer to that question. The best location for the thesis depends on your topic. You could announce your main point at the very beginning of your composition; however, you'll often find that preparing the reader with some background information is more effective. The reader may need some information about the topic or issue before she can understand your idea. If that's the case, the thesis is more appropriately placed later in the introduction.

Establish Tone

Tone is defined as the author's attitude toward his subject. In other words, tone describes the mood the writer was in when he composed the paper, a mood he transfers onto the page. The different kinds of tones include serious, scholarly, silly, humorous, lighthearted, sarcastic, angry, nostalgic, sentimental, and pleading. Writers can communicate a particular feeling about a topic through their choice of words and writing style. For instance, to create a scholarly, academic flavor, use more sophisticated vocabulary and complex sentence structures (see Chapter 3). Also, refrain from using slang or humor. In addition, you could distance yourself from the reader by not addressing him directly ("you") or referring to yourself ("I"). For example:

Their first encounter with the concept of the Dirac delta function, in an elementary course in differential equations, gives many students considerable trouble in understanding its behavior, not to mention the question of what, in fact, this "function" is. This difficulty is not surprising, considering that students' notion of limit and their physical intuition are both just being developed. My purpose in this paper is to de-mystify this useful function by providing an analysis along the lines suggested by Boyce and DiPrima and taking a close look at some physical considerations that make the properties of the delta function quite natural.[1]

The academic tone of this opening is created by long, formal sentences and sophisticated vocabulary.

For a more lighthearted or humorous flavor, you would, of course, include one or more kinds of humor (exaggeration, understatement, word play, irony, satire) in your opening. Your style would tend to be more informal, more conversational, maybe even include slang. For example, actor Bob Denver, who played shipwrecked Gilligan on the television sitcom *Gilligan's Island,* wrote a humorous piece called "How to Build a Raft." He establishes his tongue-in-cheek tone in his opening paragraph:

Being stranded on a tropical island with farm girls and movie stars isn't the worst fate a guy could face (though the Skipper wasn't my first choice as a bunkmate). But all these years later, one thing bugs me: Why is it that while we had no problem fending off cannibalistic tribes, marooned felons and even the Russian navy, we still couldn't get ourselves back to civilization? I mean, if the Professor was so smart, why couldn't he build a decent raft? What was he a professor *of?* Art history? This guy couldn't float a loan. Here's what I think: Sometimes you have to ignore the know-it-alls and take matters into your own hands. Sit right back and I'll tell you how.[2]

The humorous tone of this passage is created with the use of word play (*this guy couldn't float a loan*), funny asides (such as the one in parentheses in the first sentence), irony, an informal tone (created with words such as *guy* and *bugs*), sarcastic questions, and an echo of the television show's theme song (Sit right back . . .).

To achieve an angry tone, choose words that convey anger. For example:

New Year. Clean slate. A fresh start. No baggage. Sorry, not this century.

The calendar may have turned a page, but the athletic arena hasn't. Although the sports world remains an ever-growing land of plenty with more than enough spoils for everyone, the industry still insists on doing anything and everything to bleed the last possible penny from its misguided supporters.

Let's be clear. This isn't that stale, over-simplified argument about how the players' bloated salaries drive up ticket prices. That old saw is as passe as getting stock quotes off a ticker tape. No, this concerns certain all-too-common practices which, although certainly shameful, are, more disturbingly, disheartening. It's a wonder we have the stomach to turn to the sports page each day for our daily dose of disdain.[3]

This writer is clearly annoyed. He communicates this irritation with short, clipped sentences and sentence fragments, along with many deliberately chosen, emotionally loaded words—such as *bleed, bloated,* and *disdain*—that clearly reveal his feelings.

Different tones are appropriate for different writing tasks. A letter to your representative in Congress complaining about lack of funding for school equipment should be serious and formal. A humorous tone would be ineffective in such a letter. A memo to your supervisor requesting an adjustment to your work schedule should not reveal sarcasm or anger.

Regardless of the tone you wish to convey, establish that attitude in your opening paragraph(s) and then stick to it throughout the entire composition. If you begin with a serious, no-nonsense approach to your subject, don't suddenly switch to a humorous approach in the middle of your paper. The reader forms expectations about the writer's attitudes based on the opening. You risk confusing or frustrating her if other parts of your composition fail to fulfill those expectations.

TIP:

For more information about tone, see Chapter 11.

Interest the Reader

In today's hectic, fast-paced world, readers are busy and easily distracted by the many things competing for their attention. Good writing, therefore, must capture and hold the reader's interest from the very beginning to entice him to read and concentrate on the whole document. And that, of course, has to happen if the writing is to achieve its purpose.

So how can you pique the reader's curiosity and make him want to know more about your ideas? You can include in your opening one or more of several effective attention-getting techniques: tell a story, ask questions, establish the subject's significance, begin with a quotation, use contrast, give an example, explain your general topic, or surprise the reader.

Tell a story.   Everyone loves a good story. Narratives, real or fictional, generate immediate interest in a subject. Therefore, stories effectively draw the reader into your topic. For example, read this opening from a student's essay about the importance of wearing a helmet while riding a bicycle:

Five-year-old Johnny is riding his bicycle. He pedals up a hill, turns around, and pushes off. Suddenly going too fast, he panics. Barely controlling his speeding bike, he hits the curb and flies through the air. His head strikes a tree, knocking him unconscious. His parents rush him to the hospital, where the doctor admits him to watch for a concussion. His parents later receive a bill for a thousand dollars, but that's cheap compared to what it might have cost if he hadn't been wearing a helmet. Would your son or daughter have had a helmet on? Many children are injured in bicycle accidents, but those who wear helmets are more likely to avoid serious damage. Parents should insist their children wear helmets, which help prevent injuries and expensive medical treatment.

This opening engages the reader's interest by creating a scene that includes people participating in suspenseful events.

Another example comes from a magazine article about a new thrill-seeking trend involving dangerous games:

It was 11 P.M. on June 15, 1996, and a scene out of *American Graffiti* was heating up on the back roads of Cape Cod, Massachusetts. Patrick Swift, an 18-year-old high school junior whom friends called "Swifty," was riding with four girls in an old green car. They caravanned with friends from party to party, and most everyone had had a couple of beers—including Swifty and the 16-year-old girl behind the wheel. Maybe to impress one of them, maybe on a dare, or maybe just for a cheap thrill, Swifty decided to show off with a game he and his buddies had been playing the past few nights—car surfing.

With the car still moving, he climbed out the window and up onto the roof. Lying flat on his stomach, Swifty held on tight as the car took a sharp left turn. Then, although the car was travelling at about 33 miles an hour, he got to his knees and stood up. Suddenly, the girl driving swerved.

Swifty pitched forward into the darkness, hitting the road head-first. By the time his best friend, Chris DiGiacomo, arrived in another car minutes later, Swifty was lying facedown in a pool of blood. An ambulance pulled up as Chris, soaked in his friend's blood, tried desperately to administer CPR. But it was too late. Pam Swift would soon receive the terrible news that her son was dead.[4]

Whether your narrative is true, fictional, or hypothetical, all story openers should adhere to two important guidelines. First, they should be brief. Resist the urge to include a lot of descriptive details and instead concentrate on the plot (the events in the story). This story should not become your focus; instead, it should introduce your paper's focus. Second, the story should clearly illustrate or relate to your composition's main idea. In other words, it should have something to do with the topic you'll discuss.

TIP:

> Never begin a paper with phrases such as In this paper I am going to . . . or This essay will prove that. . . . The reader will be yawning before she finishes your first paragraph.

Ask questions. Another technique for arousing the reader's interest is to begin by asking questions that get her thinking about your topic. This method encourages the reader to directly participate by mentally answering those questions. For example, the following opening is from a magazine article:

Would you entrust your toddler into the care of a baby-sitter, even for a few minutes, who cannot hear or see your child? Would you leave your child in an environment that encourages passivity, limits creativity, and results in increased aggressive behavior? Many 1-year-olds are spending time regularly with just such a baby-sitter: the television set.[5]

A second example is from a student's essay recommending a specific film:

What do you want out of life? Do you like your job? Are you working toward a goal, or do you just clock in to pay the bills? Does your work violate your values? Do you want to make a difference? In the movie *Jerry Maguire,* the two main characters ask themselves these questions in their struggle to match their careers to their core beliefs.

Follow two guidelines when beginning with questions. First, keep each question brief and to the point. Second, don't ask too many questions. The reader is not reading your paper to be quizzed. So ask a few key questions to get him interested, and then move on to providing some answers.

Establish the significance of your subject.   Another effective way to get your reader interested involves convincing him that your subject is important. Present to the reader the data or statistics that reveal why this topic is significant and worthy of his attention. You can achieve this by stating who is affected, where, and how. For example:

When I ask people worldwide what are the three most important things in their lives, 95 percent put "family" or "family relationships" on the top-three list. Fully 75 percent put family first. Our greatest joys and our deepest heartaches surround what's happening in our family life. We want things to be right. When we sense a gap between our vision of the rich, beautiful family life we want to have and the reality of every day, we begin to feel "off track."[6]

Another example comes from a student's research paper:

Alcohol is the number one drug in America. According to the National Institute of Alcohol Abuse, over 13 million problem drinkers, including 8 million alcoholics, live in the United States. The majority of citizens believe that marijuana, cocaine, and heroin are the most dangerous drugs. However, the American Medical Association says that alcohol contributes to 100,000 deaths every year, including accidents, suicides, and homicides. The Substance Abuse and Mental Health Services Administration reports that over 3 million Americans receive treatment for their problems with alcohol. But our country's problems with alcohol will never improve until we stop excusing those who abuse this drug.

When establishing your topic's significance with data, make sure your numbers come from reputable, accurate sources. You must acknowledge those sources to increase your own credibility.

Begin with a quotation.   A quotation is another way to get your reader interested in your ideas. The best quotation is a short, clever, and thought-provoking saying, often by a famous person. For example:

The eminent 19th century American poet Ralph Waldo Emerson is quoted as saying, "A hero is no braver than an ordinary man, but he is braver five minutes longer." Luckily, the history of the United States is filled with stories of brave men and women who have given us that extra five minutes of their lives. While the merits of their deeds will always be debated, such people endure the test of time to be honored as champions of our highest national values and customs. And since it is the American people who choose to remember their lives, the process for selection is a rigorous one.[7]

Another example comes from a magazine article:

"Which comes first," someone asked Ira Gershwin, "the words or the music?" "The contract," said Gershwin. Students in the enterprise management course at the Liverpool Institute for the Performing Arts (LIPA), otherwise known as the Paul McCartney "Fame" school, will have heard that story before. Many times. Some of them may not be able to place Gershwin—doesn't he play for U-2?—but the message is loud and clear. Talent alone is not enough. To succeed in the entertainment industry these days, arguably the most competitive, hard-nosed, ruthless and insecure profession on earth, you have to be streetwise.[8]

An effective quotation is always related to your topic. It either concisely summarizes your point or leads to that main idea. When offering a quotation, always identify the speaker in order to properly credit that person.

Use contrast.   When we contrast two things, we examine their differences. This can be an appropriate method for getting the reader wondering about your topic. One type of contrast explains changes over time; in other words, you note the differences between the past and the present. The following example from a magazine article employs this type of contrast:

Raising a family is the toughest and potentially most rewarding job you'll ever have. I'm convinced it's much harder to have a successful family today, though, than it was 30 or 40 years ago. The "traditional" family of the past—a breadwinner father and a stay-at-home mother whose primary role is raising the children—is now the exception.[9]

Another type of contrast reveals the differences between the imagined and the real. For instance, this next opening from a magazine article contrasts the author's expectations with her actual experience:

Let's just say I was naive about what would be required of me as a guest teacher in Harlem. When Chandra Traavis, director of the non-profit Art Beat program, invited me to spend two days teaching writing in schools in poor areas, I jumped at the chance. I had long harbored the illusion that if I didn't have a career as a writer, I'd be a teacher. I constructed an elaborate fantasy where I'd teach until 3 P.M., then go home and write.

Standing in front of a sixth-grade class at 9 in the morning, I very quickly began to change my mind. The 11-year-olds were restless, bouncing off the walls and making merry while torturing the substitute teacher. When the sub saw I was to take over for an hour, she looked as if she'd just won a trip for two to Disneyland.[10]

A final type of contrast explains two different views, opinions, attitudes, or perspectives:

Most discussion of business ethics focuses on ethics as a constraint on profit. From this view, ethics and profit are related inversely: the more ethical a business is, the less profitable it is; the more profitable, the less ethical. Certainly, there are times when doing the morally correct thing will reduce profits. Not using an "agent" to provide bribes when doing business abroad is one example. Nonetheless, the traditional characterization of an inverse relationship between ethics and profits is only part of the story at best. A more balanced view points out that there frequently is a positive relation between ethics and profits; normally, ethics enhances the bottom line, rather than diminishing it.[11]

TIP:

> *The type of sentences you write, along with the words you choose, creates your writing style. Style is the "flavor" of your writing, which might be conversational, academic, ornate, or journalistic, to name a few. No matter what style you adopt or develop, strive to write sentences that are clear and interesting.*

Give an example. When you give an example, you describe how the experiences of one particular person illustrate your main idea. Like the story method, this technique immediately engages the reader's interest by presenting him with a real person rather than an abstract idea. For example:

My daughter Lee pays taxes at a higher marginal rate than Bill Gates. She's not an attorney, a surgeon or a recording star. She's an 18-year-old freshman at the University of Missouri who's been working and saving for college since she was in third grade.

When Lee was eight, she raised and sold her first 4-H calf. Yes, people still do that. Those 4-H projects teach responsibility: Lee has fed and watered her animals every day for ten years. At age 14, Lee also started raising flowers. From the beginning, her mother and I insisted that any profits go toward her college education. All profits

not reinvested in the Lee Hurst microconglomerate were used to purchase savings certificates at the local bank.

That was a mistake. The financial aid system for today's scan-
dalously overpriced colleges, and our federal tax code, ensure that
working and saving for college is a fool's game.[12]

Another example comes from a magazine article:

For as long as he can remember, Gordon Irlam has been shy. "I can see
it in photographs when I was young," says Irlam, 30. "I was always
hiding and looking away." Also in the picture: a mother and father
Irlam says were shy, too.

Irlam's family typifies the latest scientific findings on shyness.
Increasingly, evidence suggests babies can inherit a bashful nature just
as surely as long legs or vivid blue eyes.[13]

When giving an example, stick to the details relevant to your main
idea. Resist the urge to include information, however interesting, that
does not relate to your topic.

Explain your general topic and narrow to your specific point.   Often
the reader finds it interesting to learn more about how your one idea
relates to a broader issue or topic. So you might begin a paper with a discussion of a general subject, gradually narrowing to your specific point
about one aspect of this subject. Using this technique, you orient the
reader by showing her the "big picture" before zeroing in on one focal
point. This first example comes from a technical report:

Typhoid, hepatitis, tetanus, and cholera killed a lot of people before
humans figured out how water transmits these diseases. Since we've
come to understand this relationship, the public has pressured government to provide safe, clean water. In response, the U.S. government
established the Environmental Protection Agency, which enforces regulations to protect our water supply. One of these regulations,
Regulation 503, is designed to reduce pathogen bacteria. Government
will probably soon mandate waste pathogen reduction through aero-
bic digestion, so our company should begin to use this process now.
Doing so will demonstrate our environmental awareness to the community.

A second example is from a student's literary analysis essay:

For centuries, historians omitted the black race's experiences from textbooks. Consequently, Americans often misunderstood blacks and their problems. In his poetry, Langston Hughes attempted to reverse this trend by verbalizing his race's thoughts and feelings with what critic James Emanuel calls "ethnic passion." Hughes's poems "The Negro Speaks of Rivers" and "Negro" provide much-needed insight. In both poems, Hughes refers to both ancient and modern experiences of blacks, using allusions and imagery to strengthen the reader's understanding of black heritage.

This approach is often used in business documents such as memos and reports, where you must remind the busy reader of an overall situation or concept before he can understand your specific idea. For example, the following opening begins a memorandum:

A little over a year ago, a copier machine was installed in the first-floor workroom for the convenience of staff in that area. That copier has malfunctioned regularly, and a repairer has had to service it on a weekly basis. Overuse of this machine is causing the regular malfunctions, so we will need to implement some new guidelines for its use.

Surprise, shock, or startle the reader. Perhaps one of the best ways to pique the reader's immediate interest is to surprise, startle, or shock her. You can achieve this several ways: with an attention-getting quotation, with startling statistics, or with a fascinating or unusual fact. The following example comes from a magazine article:

"I always keep a dead calf near the house," Bernd Heinrich says over his shoulder. "Or a sheep." He is running through a Green Mountains forest in April. Leaping gullies. Vaulting boulders. Splashing through snowmelt pools. Pelting up slopes. He is off to check on a raven's nest, explaining over his shoulder how he found it—ravens feed on the carcasses he puts out, then he shadows them home.[14]

Another magazine article begins with a startling fact:

If you have been brought up pledging allegiance to the flag and the Republic for which it stands, "one nation under God, indivisible, with liberty and justice for all," there is a certain surprise in reading the Constitution and finding that it nowhere contains the word "nation" (or, for that matter, the word "God").[15]

Combining the methods.   A writer can combine different methods for stimulating interest to appeal to a variety of different readers. A student's letter to her senator provides a good example:

Our state's motto is "Iowa: A Place to Grow." Indeed, we seem to live in a progressive, prosperous state. But our problems with homelessness mock that motto. All over our state, people aimlessly wander the streets. They crowd into inadequate temporary shelters. Many live in cars and abandoned buildings. Should we dismiss them as bums and vagrants, people who don't matter? Do we rationalize that they chose this kind of life? Should we look the other way and refuse to admit to the problem? The 14,000 homeless people in Iowa cannot "grow." Their situation is caused by family problems, unemployment, scarce affordable housing, expensive rent and utilities, and lack of skills. Our state's citizens must do more to remedy these problems, for homeless people need our help. They deserve a chance to "grow," too.

This opening paragraph combines four different attention-getting techniques, including a quotation, contrast, questions, and statistics that establish the topic's significance.

TIP:

Each time you receive a graded composition back from an instructor, use her comments and suggestions to set some goals for your future papers and determine how you will achieve those goals. For example, if your instructor identifies disorganization as one of your weaknesses, resolve to write a more organized paper next time, perhaps by spending more time sorting out your ideas before you begin to write.

| EXERCISE 8.1 | *Writing Openings* |

1. For each of the following paragraphs, decide whether the writer achieved all four objectives for openings. Does the opening give enough background information? Does it state a thesis? What tone does it establish for the composition? Does it interest the reader?

   a. For many, professional football is a game of heart and soul. The sport is all about winning. A championship football team needs talent, dedication, and a good coach.

   b. I'm sick and tired of the lack of teamwork at this restaurant. All employees had better get together to fix this problem. I have a solution.

   c. Alcohol is a widely used drug in the United States because it's legal, easy to obtain, and socially acceptable. But drinkers don't understand the health risks of alcohol consumption.

   d. Though people have different musical tastes, everyone responds emotionally to music. Country, rock, classical, and rap all inspire different kinds of feelings as we listen.

   e. How do you feel after you've viewed a film? Frightened? Depressed? Happy? Movies appeal to our psychological and emotional needs.

   f. Country music is more popular than ever thanks to many talented artists. Hank Williams, Sr., Keith Whitley, Garth Brooks, and Reba McEntire are four creative leaders who have contributed to this industry's growth.

   g. I love *The Andy Griffith Show,* and I think you would enjoy it, too. You might be wondering, "Why should I watch such an old show?" Well, let me explain.

   h. In this paper, I'm going to present the reasons for the decrease in crime in the United States. Fewer crimes are being committed because of a decrease in drug traffic and a decrease in gang activity.

2. Choose three of the following thesis statements, and write two different opening paragraphs for each, using different techniques for

interesting the reader. Try to use several of the eight different techniques listed below.

Tell a story	Use contrast
Ask questions	Give an example
Establish the significance of your story	Explain your general topic
	Surprise, shock, or startle the reader
Begin with a quotation	

a. Anyone can make a perfect taco.

b. I have decided to earn a college degree for several reasons.

c. A number of factors have contributed to our current prosperous and stable American economy.

d. Renting a house and buying a house have both advantages and disadvantages.

e. When choosing a family pet, consider the required expense, maintenance, and time involved in the animal's upkeep.

f. Retirement planning should begin when you're still in your twenties.

g. To comply with the Americans with Disabilities Act, we will have to modify the doors, restrooms, and elevators in this building.

h. If a teenager drops out of school before age eighteen, he should lose his driver's license.

Chapter Summary

An effective opening always **provides background information, states your thesis, establishes your composition's tone,** and **gets the reader interested** in your topic. You can stimulate her curiosity by telling a **story,** asking **questions,** explaining the subject's **significance,** including a thought-provoking **quotation,** using **contrast,** giving an **example,** explaining your **general topic,** or **surprising** her. You can also **combine** two or more of these techniques.

Suggested Writing Activities

Practice the techniques for effective openings as you compose one or more of the following:

1. Write an essay about someone you admire.

2. Write a letter to a distant friend or relative to persuade him to visit you.

3. Write a letter to persuade a fellow student to join a particular campus club.

4. Write an essay to define the word *student*.

5. Write a proposal to suggest changes that would make your workplace environment more pleasant.

6. Write a letter to introduce and sell an item you made yourself (e.g., a craft, a food item, or an artwork).

Notes

1. Joan R. Hundhausen, "Zeroing In on the Delta Function," *The College Mathematics Journal* (January 1998), 27.

2. Bob Denver, "How to Build a Raft," *Men's Health* (March 1997), 172.

3. Wayne M. Barrett, "Greed and Hypocrisy in a Land of Plenty," *USA Today* (January 1998), 69.

4. Dan Hurley, "When Good Kids Play Dangerous Games," *Family Circle* (September 16, 1997), 56. Reprinted by permission of the author, an award-winning freelance writer based in New Jersey.

5. Nancy W. Hall, "Too Much TV?" *Parents* (March 1997), 95.

6. Stephen R. Covey, "What Makes a Happy Family?" *Family Circle* (October 7, 1997), 74.

7. Larry R. Clark, "King's Life Still Example for All," *The News Herald*, Morganton, N.C. (January 19, 1998), 4.

8. Sue Arnold, "Roll Over, Beethoven," *Smithsonian* (January 1998), 74.

9. Stephen Covey, "How Any Family Can Be Happy," *USA Weekend* (September 26–28, 1997), 10.

10. Veronica Chambers, "Good Kids in Bad Situations," *USA Weekend* (September 12–14, 1997), 18.

11. Norman E. Bowie, "Companies Are Discovering the Value of Ethics," *USA Today* (January 1998), 22.

12. Blake Hurst, "My Kid's College Fund Blues," *Reader's Digest* (November 1997), 45, 48.

13. Melissa Hendricks, "Why So Shy?" *USA Weekend* (September 19–21, 1997), 12.

14. Richard Wolkomir, "From Twigs to Ravens, Nothing Escapes the Notice of Bernd Heinrich," *Smithsonian* (November 1997), 94.

15. Robert Wernick, "Chief Justice Marshall Takes the Law in Hand," *Smithsonian* (November 1998), 157.

NINE

Effective Closings

People are accustomed to clear endings. We don't like to hang up the phone until both speakers have said goodbye. We like predictable endings in our popular music: either a crescendo building to a resounding climax, a final long note, or repetition while the tune fades. We like our movies and television shows to end satisfactorily, with all of the loose ends tied up and all of the characters getting the rewards or punishments they deserve.

As readers, too, we expect clear, satisfactory endings in compositions. We want to feel a sense of closure when we finish reading. We want thoughts and ideas to be wrapped up neatly and logically.

As writers, though, we often find closure difficult to achieve. Once we've thoroughly explained all of our ideas, we're not sure how to end because we feel as though we've said all we wanted to say. So we're tempted to simply tack on a little summary to conclude a paper, one that merely repeats the points we've already discussed. Repetition and summary, though, tend to be dull, lifeless ways to end a paper. On the other hand, the closing is not the place to introduce brand-new ideas either.

A better way to end the compositions you write is to use your closing paragraph(s) as an opportunity to share with the reader the consequences or implications of your ideas. Assume that you've convinced your reader to accept the idea or belief stated in your thesis, and then ask yourself, "So what?" The answer to that question then becomes your closing. For example, in a memo that describes required hand-washing procedures for employees who handle food, your closing might explain how this requirement will increase customer confidence, reduce complaints, and, therefore, ultimately increase the company's profits. In a research paper that informs the reader about a new cancer drug, you might predict how this drug will change the future of treatment for this disease. In a letter to a company complaining about a faulty product, you might suggest that the manufacturer replace the item or refund your money.

When deciding how to explain consequences or implications, writers can choose from five effective techniques for concluding their compositions: describe effects, make predictions, make recommendations, complete a circle, or ask questions to keep the reader thinking.

Describe Effects

One way to end a composition is to describe the effects of your ideas. These effects could be short-term, long-term, or both. Upon completing your paper, ask yourself this question: "Now that I've established my point about this topic, what changes will (or did) it cause?" For example, in a report about a new computer technology, the closing paragraph might mention all of the ways it's changing business and industry. In a literary analysis essay about a specific poet's technique, you could explain how this technique influenced other writers.

One example is from a journal article that describes the author's experience in Jamaica at a workshop for potters. After describing the week's events, she ends with:

After carefully packing our pots and having a final meal on the beach, we left the next day, inspired to get back to our own studios and find opportunities to wood fire again. To me, the most striking aspect of this workshop was the intense energy and excitement created by a group of people coming together from different clay environments with one common love—working with clay. Strong friendships were developed. Meeting with local artists and educators gave everyday insights into the rich and wonderful Jamaican culture. Whether we work in Jamaica, Norway, Utah or New York City, we all share similar goals, pleasures and difficulties when working/making pots. To learn about techniques and processes of other potters around the world is to benefit from their experiences—both victorious and frustrating. It was a fulfilling exchange of ideas.[1]

After describing her trip, this author concludes by mentioning the effects (friendships, insights into Jamaican culture, exchange of ideas about the craft) of her experiences.

Another example comes from a letter to the editor of a newspaper. The author, who heads the Peace Corps, wrote to explain his organization's history and current project. He concludes his letter with a paragraph summarizing the beneficial effects of this project:

The young people who participate in Peace Corps Day will learn a great deal about people from around the world. What they may not realize, however, is that they will also be building the bridges of friendship and understanding that are the foundation of peace among nations.[2]

A third example is from a student's report about computer-aided interior design. After explaining how computers assist the design process and describing several specific programs, the writer concludes the report with a paragraph that discusses the effects of these programs:

Interior designers already use computer programs extensively. Many design and architectural firms have even abandoned traditional drafting methods, preferring the simplicity, speed, and cost-effectiveness of computer programs. In return, the computer industry continues to develop sophisticated new programs to help the building industry fulfill its clients' needs.

TIP:

Even professional writers struggle to get the words right.

Make Predictions

Another effective way to conclude some compositions is to make some predictions for the future. These predictions should arise naturally out of the information you've presented in your paper. For instance, in a letter to a representative in Congress about the poor condition of roads near your home, you might speculate that more accidents and injuries will occur if these roads are not repaired. In a report about mortgage loan rates for your business class, you might make some predictions about future trends.

One example comes from a magazine article about the new common European currency called the "euro." The article covers the benefits of the euro, a description of the coins and paper currency, and expectations about the transition period. Finally, to conclude the composition, the author ends with a look at the future:

> The euro has all the makings of a major global currency. Will it turn out to be a rival of the dollar? Will the euro gain additional prestige as a so-called reserve currency? It's certainly possible. But as an official at the New York Federal Reserve Bank (whose vaults are stacked with gold) recently put it, "Two-thirds of all U.S. currency in circulation is overseas." On that basis alone, if there is a currency competition, the dollar will be a formidable rival.[3]

Another example comes from a student's research report about a Japanese approach to business management called *Kaizen*. The report defines the term, describes how it works, and then discusses advantages and disadvantages of this method. To conclude, the author mentions some effects of this approach and then ends with a prediction:

> When the automotive industry uses the Kaizen teamwork method, everyone—from employees to managers to customers—benefits. Kaizen saves time and money for everyone involved. In the future, as more plants implement the Kaizen team approach, production and profits will rise.

A final example is from a newspaper editorial about the increasing number of Muslims in America:

Newsweek said Muslims are emerging in the professions and as a cohesive voting block. U.S. Muslims, it concludes, may become a force to be reckoned with. Within the decade it may not be thirst for Mideast oil that pushes Washington to court the Arabs, but a wealthy, vocal lobby right in its midst.[4]

Make Recommendations

A third way to present the implications of your ideas is to recommend that the reader do something in response to your ideas. You might ask that he change a belief or a behavior. For instance, you could suggest that he write a letter, join a group, buy a particular product, or make a certain decision. In an editorial about why the reader should help save a historic battleship, you might ask him to donate money or to volunteer his time to an organization. Following a review of a new film, you could recommend that the reader go see it.

The following example is from a student's research paper about horse abuse. The author discusses the different types of abuse and their effects. To conclude, she recommends a course of action for the reader:

Can we stop horse abuse? Yes, but we'll have to speak out. Silent disapproval isn't enough. If you see a horse being abused, call your local animal welfare agency, a group that can remove the animal from its abuser. Join a humane society, work to make penalties more harsh, and write letters to your legislators. Finally, boycott rodeos, which perpetuate the abuse. Protest to the rodeo's sponsors, write letters to your newspaper's editor, and organize a demonstration to make people aware of the suffering.

This next example comes from a letter to the editor of a newspaper. The author advocates the election of a particular candidate to the local school board. After describing the candidate's qualifications and merits, she concludes with:

Please consider the future of the schools in our county and do your part to elect a professional, seasoned educator who knows first-hand the educational needs of our young people. We are facing a period of tremendous growth that requires foresight, knowledge, and experience. Ernest Stone possesses those qualities.[5]

A memo offers another example of the recommendation technique. After describing and evaluating the features of three different fax machines, the writer ends with a paragraph that states his recommendation about which machine the reader should purchase:

Because the Intellifax 615 has the same features as the other two machines but costs less money, it is clearly the better buy. It will serve the Legal Department's needs, so I recommend that we purchase it.

> **TIP:**
>
> *Don't ever throw away prewriting, outlines, or drafts of a document until it is complete and delivered to your reader.*

Complete a Circle

Another good technique for wrapping up a paper involves referring to something you mentioned earlier in the composition, often in the opening, thus circling back and closing a loop. This method leaves the reader feeling as though the ending is tied neatly to the beginning. One example comes from a magazine article about Olympic ice skater Tara Lipinski. The opening paragraph mentions Tara's love of vacations at Walt Disney World. Then the article goes on to describe the triumphs and setbacks in her last year of competition. The article ends with the following paragraph:

Lipinski knows who she is. "I look so young that if I tried to look 19, it would be unbelievable," she says. Her long program [for Olympic competition], appropriately enough, is about a young girl's race to live her dreams. After her stunning fall at the nationals, Tara fought back into second place and onto the Olympic team—"my dream my whole life," she said afterward. "I plan to make more dreams come true." Just like Disney.[6]

That last reference to Disney brings the composition back to where it began, leaving the reader with a satisfying sense of closure.

A second example comes from a humorous newspaper article. The author explains her six New Year's Resolutions: lose weight, stop acting like a teacher out in public, go to bed early and get up early, stop procrastinating, have more scruples, and stop exaggerating. Her concluding paragraph is:

Right now I'm going to go make myself a ham sandwich. Just as soon as I yell at those noisy teenagers walking down the street. You'd think people wouldn't be up at this hour of the morning. I might then grade those quizzes from Jan. 6. I have two thousand of them to grade and that is no exaggeration. . . .[7]

This closing not only illustrates each of the resolutions described earlier in the article, it also humorously points out that the author is already ignoring them!

One final example is from a student's research paper about school uniforms. The writer begins his paper with an anecdote about John, a high school senior shot and killed by another student who steals his expensive athletic shoes. To conclude the paper, he circles back to his beginning:

If he had been wearing a uniform, John would not have been murdered for his shoes. Instead, he would have lived to benefit from a school that promoted self-esteem and unity for all of its students through the removal of economic class distinctions. He would have lived to complete his education in a place that chose a standardized dress code to create a safe atmosphere for success.

TIP:

For more about techniques for effective openings, see Chapter 8.

Ask Questions

One final technique for ending a paper involves asking the reader questions. These questions ask your reader to keep thinking about your topic even after she has finished reading the paper. For instance, in an essay urging Southern institutions to retire their rebel flags, the writer might end with a question such as:

Even though this symbol may have historical value, shouldn't we also consider the pain and rage it recalls in many of those forced to watch it flutter in the breeze?

This example comes from a student's essay that argues the merits of a television show called *Rescue 911*. She concludes her essay with:

Rescue 911 saves lives every day by showing us what to do when someone is injured in an accident. One day, one of this show's viewers might save me or one of my family members. Or could the next life saved be yours or your child's?

Another example is from a magazine article about musicians who possess "absolute pitch," the ability to correctly identify any musical note they hear. The article discusses the origins, benefits, and skeptical attitude of some regarding this talent. The author concludes with the following paragraph:

There is an old saying at the poker table that winners count their money while losers cry, "Deal the cards." . . . Could it be that all those who claim the benefits of absolute pitch (some undeniably real) are also exercising a strategy to gain higher ground over those perceived to be less fortunate? And if I had perfect pitch, wouldn't I be right there with them?[8]

A letter to the editor offers a final example. A high school teacher responds to the blame placed on teachers for students' low test scores. He concludes with:

I am accountable for my students' progress, and I feel that I should be. Yet, how does the state legislature so blatantly overlook the culpability of students and parents when end-of-course results are not what they should be?[9]

| EXERCISE 9.1 | *Writing Closings* |

For each of the following brief compositions, write two different closing paragraphs using two different techniques listed below.

Describe effects   Complete a circle
Make predictions   Ask questions
Make recommendations

Security and Privacy on the Internet

A rapidly growing network of computers forms what we call the Internet. In the last few years, message traffic across the Internet has dramatically increased. Users send electronic mail, transfer files, and make payments. Many are unaware, though, that their personal and private information could become public record on the Internet. For instance, your record of traffic violations or the amount of your inheritance may be accessible to everyone. Such security and privacy issues should concern all Internet users.

Security for Internet users is not easy to guarantee, especially for electronic payments. Software companies are working on ways to make payment information difficult to steal or counterfeit. In particular, they're developing encryption, which encodes data for protection and authenticity. So far, though, encryption isn't foolproof. Encoded messages can still be duplicated and used by someone posing as the original sender. For example, if a consumer uses her credit card to buy a book via the Internet, the credit card information might be transferred through several different computers before it gets to the bookseller. Hacks can intercept the information and then steal the credit card number. Therefore, Internet payments are still not completely safe.

Protecting privacy is another problem on the Internet. A computer user can find out all kinds of information about you without ever leaving the keyboard. Public records are easily accessible to anyone with a computer modem. Furthermore, users can look up social security numbers, bank account balances, tax returns, or other personal data.

Many people surf the World Wide Web believing that their movements are private and anonymous. However, every time you retrieve a file, send an e-mail, or access a specific web site, a record is created of that action. These records allow others to track where you've been, which, of course, violates your privacy.

Bloom for Joy

"Every once in a while somebody will come in and comment on how beautiful they are," he said. "They just give everybody a smile."

—Burke County gas station attendant,
on wildflowers planted by the state

Indeed, the wildflowers on North Carolina's roads do generate a lot of smiles. They're a pleasure to look at, a reminder that beauty can be a bit unkempt, a relief from the regularity and demands of the road— and a break from the notion that government services must always be regimented, necessary and soullessly efficient.

These wildflowers aren't free, of course. There is $800,000 from federal beautification funds and vanity license plates. And people like Donna Garrison, the roadside environmental engineer for the N.C. Department of Transportation . . . work hard so that drivers can enjoy a bit of beauty. State folks take pride in winning the competition judged by the Garden Club of North Carolina. She's careful to warn that the flowers also attract things like bees and copperheads.

But the effect of the blooms is wonderful. . . . The delight at the flowers is instructive. Government ought to reflect the people as well as serve them. Life is not all forms and order. There ought to be room for the delightful and the grand as well as the strictly necessary.[10]

MEMORANDUM

To:	Department Heads
	Chief Fiscal Officers
From:	Edward Renfrow, State Controller
Date:	October 23, 1996
Subject:	Potential Telephone Fraud

Please make sure your employees are aware that returning telephone calls to the 809 area code creates the potential for incurring very expensive toll charges. The 809 area code looks like a normal telephone area code within the United States, but, in fact, it is utilized for telephone calls to the Caribbean. Telephone calls to the 809 area code are billed at international rates and they may include surcharges. These charges could be as high as *$25.00 per minute.* Individuals and companies have developed schemes that trap the unsuspecting into making calls to the 809 area code at these outlandish rates to the caller. Some of the scams utilize, but are not limited to, the following practices:

- A company identifying itself as "Global Communications" has been sending unsolicited and tersely worded messages and letters to individuals threatening legal action unless the recipient pays an unspecified overdue account. The message then gives a name and telephone number in the 809 area code to call for further information.

- A message is left on voice mail or an answering machine claiming to have information on a family member who is ill, has died, or has been arrested. The message leaves an 809 area code and telephone number for the person to call.

- A message or letter promises a prize to the recipient if he calls the 809 area code and telephone number to collect the prize.

- Messages are sent to pagers for the recipient to call an 809 area code and telephone number.

The Federal Communications Commission requires U.S. carriers to state up front the cost of a pay-per-call service, but there is nothing the U.S. government can do about foreign companies operating in the Caribbean. Every government employee needs to be aware of this situation.[11]

Chapter Summary

An effective ending in a composition presents the consequences or implications of the writer's idea. You can achieve this by **describing**

effects, making predictions or recommendations, completing a circle you began in the opening, or **asking questions** to keep the reader thinking.

Suggested Writing Activities

As you write one or more of the following compositions, experiment with different ways to end them:

1. Write an essay about stress-relief techniques that work for you.

2. Write a report summarizing the performance of your favorite sports team over the last year.

3. Write a letter to your college's dean of students to propose a needed service on campus.

4. Write instructions for how to register for a class at the college you attend.

5. Write an essay to argue that a particular invention has been the most important innovation of this century.

6. Write a letter to praise a company for its product or service.

Notes

1. Kathy King with Jeff Cox, "Wood Firing in Jamaica," *Ceramics Monthly* (January 1996), 35.

2. Mark D. Gearan, "Letters to the Editor," *The News Herald*, Morganton, N.C. (March 5, 1998), 4A.

3. Paul Burnham Finney, "Making Sense of the Euro," *The New Yorker* (April 12, 1999), 41.

4. Mary Dejevsky, "Muslims Overtaking Jews in United States," *Charlotte Observer*, Charlotte, N.C. (March 30, 1998), 11A.

5. Vivian Wilson, "Letters to the Editor," *The News Herald*, Morganton, N.C. (October 27, 1997), 4.

6. "Beautiful Dreamer," *Newsweek* (February 9, 1998), 62.

7. Kaye Fish, "Resolutions Losing Steam by Now," *The News Herald*, Morganton, N.C. (January 25, 1998), 4A.

8. Bernard Holland, "'Tis a Gift to Be Perfect. Or Is It?" *The New York Times* (March 1, 1998), Section 2, 31.

9. Jeff Hamilton, "The Observer Forum," *Charlotte Observer*, Charlotte, N.C. (March 30, 1998), 10A. Reprinted with permission from the *Charlotte Observer*.

10. "Bloom for Joy," *Charlotte Observer*, Charlotte, N.C. (June 2, 1998), 10A. Reprinted by permission of the *Charlotte Observer*.

11. Edward Renfrow, North Carolina Office of the State Controller. Memorandum to all state employees (October 23, 1996). Reprinted by permission.

TEN

Confidence and Assertiveness

*E*ffective writing is always confident and assertive. Confidence is the sincere belief in the ideas being communicated. Assertiveness is the ability to declare these ideas as true and valid. A reader will often evaluate the writer's thoughts based on how confidently she presents them. If the composition reveals doubt, timidity, or uncertainty, the reader may reject its ideas because he's not sure the *writer* even believes them. Thus, the document will not convince the reader and will not achieve its purpose.

Of course, to write confidently, you must first have confidence in your ideas. If you are unsure about your topic, if you don't fully understand it, or if you harbor any doubts about your thesis or main points, this uncertainty will surface in your writing. So you must take the time to think through your ideas, subject them to intense scrutiny, test their validity, and discuss them with people who disagree or hold differing viewpoints. Only when you truly believe in your idea can you communicate it assertively to a reader.

This chapter discusses four ways to achieve confident writing: by avoiding certain apologetic or hedging phrases, by choosing confident words, by stating ideas using more confident, declarative sentence structure, and by using certain typefaces to emphasize and reinforce ideas.

Avoid Hedging, Apologies, and Disclaimers

Adding certain phrases to your sentences will result in writing that seems timid and unsure. The term *hedging* effectively describes the first group of phrases. *To hedge* means to avoid a firm commitment by making statements that allow you to withdraw or escape from your position. Some common hedging phrases are:

> It seems to me
>
> I think
>
> I believe
>
> I feel that
>
> In my opinion

All of these phrases inject a note of uncertainty into your writing by calling attention to the fact that these are your thoughts alone. They indirectly suggest *your* thoughts do not necessarily represent prevailing wisdom. Therefore, they call into question the validity of your statements.

Furthermore, hedging phrases are redundant, adding unnecessary words to your sentences. Because you are writing the statement, you obviously believe it, think it, or feel it; therefore, it's unnecessary to say so.

Note how the revisions of the following examples result in much more confident statements:

HEDGING: *I believe that* exposing a child to cigarette smoke in his own home violates his civil rights.

MORE CONFIDENT: Exposing a child to cigarette smoke in his own home violates his civil rights.

HEDGING: *I think* the electoral college is valuable even though it doesn't reflect what the citizens really want. [This statement is also contradictory, further destroying its confidence.]

MORE CONFIDENT: The electoral college does not always reflect what the citizens really want.

HEDGING: Marianne Moore's poem "A Jelly Fish" symbolizes the search for faith, *as I interpret it.*

MORE CONFIDENT: Marianne Moore's poem "A Jelly Fish" symbolizes the search for faith.

HEDGING: *I feel* if our state lowered the legal drinking age, we would be better off! Today people use a designated driver, so if the drinking age were 18, *I feel that* fewer accidents would occur. Someone would take the intoxicated person home. *I could possibly be wrong though!* [In addition to all of the hedging phrases, note the writer's questionable logic.]

MORE CONFIDENT: If our state lowered the legal drinking age, we would be better off! Today even teenagers use a designated driver, and they would continue to do so even if the drinking age were 18. Someone could drive the intoxicated person home.

Another type of hedging word is the qualifier, a word that limits an idea or makes it less positive. Common qualifiers include *probably, maybe, seems,* and *some.* Overuse of these words results in timid, wimpy writing. Notice how the removal of qualifiers in the following statements increases their confidence:

HEDGING: Robert E. Lee was *probably* one of the most capable military commanders in history.

MORE CONFIDENT: Robert E. Lee was one of the most capable military commanders in history.

HEDGING: *Sometimes* when a football team performs poorly, maybe the individual players lack talent.

MORE CONFIDENT: When a football team performs poorly, a lack of individual talent is often to blame.

HEDGING: Stubbornness *can be viewed* as a *rather* asinine quality in a person.

MORE CONFIDENT: Stubborn people are asinine.

TIP:

Your ideas and opinions matter. You have a right to state what you believe.

Hedging also includes fence-sitting, or refusing to take a stand about an issue. If you're "sitting on the fence," undecided about which side to choose, you haven't yet made a commitment one way or the other. This indecision will reduce the reader's confidence in your writing. As the following statements illustrate, when the writer hasn't made a firm decision about her topic, her statements will clearly reveal her uncertainty:

HEDGING: Censorship may or may not be the solution, but the problem is certainly there.

MORE CONFIDENT: Censorship is not the solution to the problem.

HEDGING: Some type of action needs to be taken to fix this situation. [What action? Taken by whom? This writer needs to give more thought to his topic before he can improve this sentence.]

Apologies and disclaimers are another group of phrases that undermine the confidence of writing. An apology is an acknowledgment of some weakness or deficiency, usually in the writer's understanding or information. Similarly, *to disclaim* means "to disown," which involves rejecting responsibility for a statement. Common apologies and disclaimers include phrases such as:

I don't really know much about this, but . . .

I'm not really sure, but . . .

I'm no expert, but . . .

I don't have a degree in this, but . . .

By including such phrases, you immediately destroy your credibility for the reader, who will probably dismiss your thoughts as unreliable. If you really don't know what you need to know about the topic, *don't write about it until you gather more information*. On the other hand, if you *do* understand the topic and can offer appropriate evidence to support your ideas, present those ideas confidently.

Don't water down your writing with hedging, apologies, and disclaimers. Instead, state your idea as though it is truth that everyone accepts (or should accept). When you write, take a stand, believe in your position, and avoid phrases that cast doubt upon your viewpoint.

Choose Assertive Words

To achieve an assertive style, choose assertive words. Use bold, even forceful words to clearly reveal the strength of your convictions. For example, read the following letter to a magazine editor. The author of this letter feels very strongly about an article on the American Civil Liberties Union (ACLU) published by the magazine:

I am *appalled* that you would publish such a favorable article about the ACLU. This is a *slap in the face* of *every* law-abiding citizen in the United States. The ACLU is an *anti-American, anti-religion* and *anti-government* organization that would like to see the *downfall* of our society. Their not-so-well-known hidden motives are to *destroy* the U.S. Constitution through the courts and juries, establishing laws of their own choosing via liberal court decisions that would *never* be passed under normal congressional procedures.

Your headline "The ACLU Defends Everybody" is not true: they do not defend me; they *attack* me, the United States of America and the millions of citizens who fought, bled and died for this country.[1]

This writer assertively communicates his viewpoint by choosing words that effectively reveal his strong feelings about his subject.

Selecting bold, assertive words requires consideration of two qualities. First, the right word is the most specific word. Look at the following list:

plain

unattractive

ugly

hideous

If you want to state your judgment about the appearance of a new building in your community, you should choose the adjective in the list above that most specifically communicates your opinion. Chapter 2 discusses specific word choices in more detail.

After you've narrowed your choices based on their specificity, the second step involves considering any connotations attached to those words. The connotative meaning of a word refers to the emotion or feeling we have assigned to that word beyond its denotative, or dictionary, definition. Many words have taken on either positive or negative connotations that the writer should use in order to help convey his opinions. For example, compare the words *police officer* and *cop*. Although they refer to the same individual, the latter word has a derogatory, disrespectful connotation.

In the list above, the first two words (*plain* and *unattractive*) are gentle, even euphemistic choices. The last two words (*ugly* and *hideous*) are blunt and much more harsh. If you really hate the new building, they'd be the best choices for revealing your feelings.

Now consider this list:

could

should

must

Each verb in this list is a little more forceful than the one that comes before. In the statements below, the word *could* presents the idea as a questionable suggestion, *should* makes it a little more assertive by injecting the writer's opinion, and *must* is the most assertive, leaving out any room for debate:

TIMID:	We *could* ask for a raise.
MORE CONFIDENT:	We *should* ask for a raise.
MOST ASSERTIVE:	We *must* ask for a raise.

Note how the assertive verbs in the following passage from a student's essay create an authoritative, confident tone:

Horses *demand* a lot of work. A potential horse owner *must be* willing to engage in physical labor. Horses *are not* animals you can simply let loose into the backyard. They *need* regular grooming, exercise, and veterinary care. However, a dedicated owner who takes care of her horse *will be rewarded* with years of pleasure.

Finally, consider inserting into your writing some assertive adverbs that strengthen the confidence of your statements. These adverbs include words such as *clearly, obviously, definitely,* and *of course.* Such words, as the following statements illustrate, leave no room for doubt about your confidence in the idea:

Property owners who clear-cut *definitely* must replant to maintain the land's value for the future.

We oppose the construction of this airport because there are *absolutely* no demographics to support a need for this facility.[2]

The following examples both illustrate how bold word choices (in italics) of all parts of speech create assertive writing. The first, from a newspaper editorial, is a response to another editorial that proclaimed parents to be responsible for their children's acts of violence:

Your *intense prejudice* against responsible gun ownership is nothing more than another *hysterical* attempt to promote and encourage the *disarmed and helpless* citizenry that criminals rely upon for success in their *predatory* habits.[3]

This next example is from a book:

It is *absolutely pathetic* that high-school and college competitions on television, such as *College Bowl,* reward the kind of *mindless* recall of trivia that will later produce a thinker who *is good for practically nothing* except such games. The National Geography Bee, the National Spelling Bee, and other such contests are similar examples of the *mindlessness* for which we reward our children.[4]

Now consider the following examples, which become much more assertive with a few deletions and additions:

NOT CONFIDENT: *I personally think that* a school that offers bilingual education *might be* better than a school that refuses to offer any assistance to its non-English-speaking students.

MORE ASSERTIVE: A school that offers bilingual education *is clearly* better than a school that refuses assistance to its non-English-speaking students.

NOT CONFIDENT:	*I feel that* if I am hired, *I could be* an asset to your company because of my management experience.
MORE ASSERTIVE:	My management experience *will benefit* your company.
NOT CONFIDENT:	*Perhaps it is none of my business to comment* on the debate about rezoning the property.
MORE ASSERTIVE:	*I want to comment* on the debate about rezoning the property.
NOT CONFIDENT:	Her speech *seemed to* cover all of the important points, but *it felt like* she was no longer excited about her topic. She *appeared to be* reciting the same old points with little enthusiasm. *I really* didn't fully understand some of her ideas. *I don't think* she gave any examples or illustrations to support her points. The speech was dull, *I thought. In my opinion,* listening to this speech *might be* compared to eating dry toast with no butter.
MORE ASSERTIVE:	Her speech covered all of the important points, but she was *obviously* no longer excited about her topic. She recited the same old points with little enthusiasm. I did not fully understand some of her ideas because she offered no examples or illustrations to support her points. The speech was *definitely* dull; it *reminded me* of eating dry toast with no butter.

As you search for more assertive words when you write, beware of two specific dangers: (1) overgeneralizing, and (2) insulting the reader. While you should phrase your ideas as the truth, you also should avoid unfair or inaccurate generalizations and absolutes. In particular, be careful with words such as *all, always, never, none, no one, every,* and *everyone.* These words leave no room for exceptions, so they might make your statement untrue. The following statements from student papers are invalid because of their overgeneralizing words:

The number one goal of *every* hard-working American is to earn money.

Most parents are too busy with their own lives to devote time to their children.

In your choice of words that most accurately convey your attitudes and opinions, you must also avoid insensitive words or phrases, ones that might offend, insult, or ignore the reader and her needs. Chapter 11 fully discusses this topic.

> **TIP:**
>
> *Avoid including too many effusive adjectives in your writing. Words such as* really, truly, marvelous, wonderful, *and* fantastic *add an exaggerated quality and undermine your authoritative tone.*

Write Assertive Sentences

Another technique for writing more assertive prose is to phrase the vast majority of your ideas using assertive sentence structure. The four different kinds of sentences are declarative, imperative, interrogative, and exclamatory. A declarative sentence, which ends with a period, declares or states with authority an idea: *You'll need to read Chapter 1 by next week.* An imperative sentence is one that gives a command or makes a request: *Please read Chapter 1 by next week.* It, too, ends with a period. An interrogative sentence asks a question and ends with a question mark: *Can you read Chapter 1 by next week?* An exclamatory sentence exclaims an idea, expressing it as a strong feeling: *Chapter 1 will delight and amaze you!* This type of sentence ends with an exclamation point.

The declarative and imperative sentence types express ideas most assertively. The period at the end of a statement adds a note of finality and truth. So by relying predominantly on this sentence structure, you will write more assertive prose.

In contrast, the interrogative sentence, because it's a question, adds a note of uncertainty or indecisiveness to your writing. For example, notice how the following example becomes much more assertive when converted to an imperative sentence:

INTERROGATIVE: Why have kids if you don't want to stay home and take care of them?[5]

IMPERATIVE: Don't have kids if you don't want to stay home and take care of them.

While you can insert an occasional question into a document, you should not overuse this type of sentence. When you ask a question of the reader, make sure you always answer it with a declarative statement. One exception to this rule is the rhetorical question you ask in a closing paragraph to keep the reader thinking about the topic even after he puts down your composition.

The exclamatory sentence may seem assertive, for the exclamation point at its end emphasizes the idea. When used sparingly, it can be effective in calling attention to a particular point. However, when overused, it produces the opposite effect. Too many statements punctuated as exclamations will add a note of overreaction, even hysteria, to your writing that the reader may interpret as insecurity or emotionalism. For example, read the following letter to a newspaper editor, which includes too many exclamatory sentences:

The increase in business at the chicken processing plant may be good for the company, but it's a NIGHTMARE for ALL of its unfortunate neighbors! People praise the plant for the additional jobs it has brought to this town. However, they don't realize that the company has RUINED our neighborhood with 24-hour-a-day squawking, traffic, and the disgusting odor of chicken feces!! The people who live on all sides of the plant need our fresh air and our peace and quiet. We long to be able to sit outside on our porches or in our yards without being subjected to the noise and stench! We'd like to invite the public to visit our homes and see if you'd like this mess in your backyard! This type of business does NOT belong in a residential neighborhood!! It needs to relocate to an isolated area where it can't pollute the lives of hard-working homeowners!!!

Almost every sentence in this letter ends with one or more exclamation points. The writer intends to emphasize the anger and frustration he's feeling, but instead, he seems frantic.

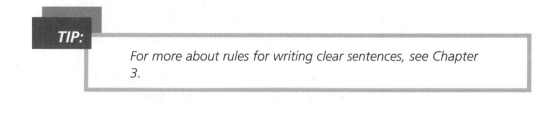

TIP:

For more about rules for writing clear sentences, see Chapter 3.

If you're using assertive words, as discussed in the previous section, you will not need to rely on exclamatory sentences to communicate the strength of your convictions.

Use Varying Typefaces for Emphasis

If even after using assertive words in declarative sentences you still feel compelled to further emphasize your ideas, use varying typefaces to make words, phrases, or whole sentences stand out. In the editorial letter in the previous section, for example, the writer capitalizes several words (*NIGHTMARE, ALL, RUINED, NOT*) to stress certain points. You can also use **bold print,** underlining, or *italics* to achieve the same effect.

However, use these typefaces sparingly and only to emphasize one specific phrase or thought. Don't type an entire document using all capital letters in an attempt to stress your ideas; the result will be a document that's difficult to read. When overused, emphasizing typefaces can have the same negative effect as too many exclamation points.

EXERCISE 10.1   *Assertive Statements*

Rewrite the following sentences to make them more assertive.

1. It seemed to me that their "concerns" were actually prejudice.[6]

2. My brother and I enjoy a close relationship; I guess that's because we've faced many hardships together.

3. Profanity on television is something that I don't strongly approve of.

4. Would it not be better to pay thirty dollars for a helmet rather than a thousand dollars for a trip to the hospital?

5. If you've read the book, maybe you agree with my opinion.

6. I personally feel the movie is very violent.

7. The physical characteristics of a wolverine are somewhat unique compared to other animals.

8. With my education and computer experience, I believe I can become a valuable member of your team.

9. Don't people realize that they could be victims of circumstances that force them to go on welfare, too? Don't they realize that many people who use food stamps aren't happy about their predicament?

10. Parents, DON'T JUST SIT THERE! JOIN THE CAUSE! HELP US GET AFFORDABLE MEDICAL INSURANCE FOR OUR CHILDREN!

11. I don't know about you, but I think we live in a pretty dangerous world.

Chapter Summary

State your ideas confidently and assertively. **Don't hedge, apologize,** or **tack disclaimers** onto your sentences. Choose **assertive words,** and write **declarative and imperative sentences.** Finally, occasionally use **different typefaces** to emphasize your ideas.

Suggested Writing Activities

As you write one or more of the following compositions, avoid hedging, apologies, and disclaimers. Also, choose assertive words and sentence structure.

1. Write a letter to your local newspaper editor to argue for a needed change in your community.

2. Write an editorial to either support or oppose a particular project in your community.

3. Write a summary of the events or ideas in a poem.

4. Argue for or against a particular type of television show (e.g., talk shows, soap operas, cartoons).

5. Write a letter to complain about the poor quality of a product or service.

6. Write a memo to your supervisor to request an increase in pay.

Notes

1. T. Med Hogg, "Letters to the Editor," *Smithsonian* (March 1998), 18. Reprinted by permission of the author.

2. Charles W. Walker, Sr., "Letters to the Editor," *The News Herald*, Morganton, N.C. (June 14, 1998), 5A.

3. Steve Towe, "Whatever Happened to Individual Responsibility?" *Asheville Citizen-Times* (June 4, 1998), A7.

4. Robert J. Sternberg, *Successful Intelligence* (New York: Simon & Schuster, 1996), 100–101.

5. Colleene Johnson, "Letters," *Time* (February 24, 1997), 6.

6. Gabriela Kuntz, "My Spanish Standoff," *Newsweek* (May 4, 1998), 22.

ELEVEN

Sensitivity and Tact

*L*et's say you arrived home one day to find the following note taped to your front door:

Dear Neighbor,
Your stupid dog is a menace to this neighborhood. He barks all the time and digs up my flowers. Any moron knows that dogs have to be kept on a leash. Tie up the mutt or I'll call the dog pound to pick him up.

> Sincerely,
> I. M. Irate

What would be your reaction to this note? You'd probably be angry and defensive, even if you were in the wrong. Even if you are breaking the law, this note is probably not going to get you to tie up your dog. Because Mr. Irate insults both you and your dog with words such as *stupid, menace, moron,* and *mutt,* you won't be inclined to do what he wants, even if he has a valid request.

Writers should always strive to phrase their ideas and opinions with confidence, as Chapter 10 recommends. However, we must balance this assertiveness with an awareness of our reader's needs, goals, and feelings. Though we do want to present our thoughts unequivocally, we must also take care to avoid offending or insulting the reader, for doing so will cause her to reject our ideas. Instead, we want to make sure we state our ideas with sensitivity and tact, always tailoring a composition to the specific reader.

This means that a careful consideration of the reader must be an important step in planning any composition. First, a writer needs to think about his reader's priorities. For instance, a writer who wants his neighbor to tie up his dog should keep in mind that this neighbor might let his pet run free because he cares for the animal and doesn't want him to live his life on the end of a chain. Yet, he probably wants to keep his pet alive and out of harm's way. Of course, he may not tie up the dog simply because it's just easier for him to let the animal loose.

Next, identify the reader's needs. Ask yourself why he might find your ideas useful or interesting. In the case of the loose dog letter, perhaps the reader doesn't even know that his dog disturbs his neighbors. So one of his needs is information about the problem. Also, he could probably use some suggestions about solutions to the problem.

Then, consider any objections he might have to your ideas. The owner of the loose dog might feel that chaining an animal is cruel. He may not be able to afford other options, such as a dog pen. He might also object to the stress of having to listen to his confined dog bark and whine. How will you address and overcome these concerns?

Finally, what language will most sensitively convince him to believe you? Your conclusions about your reader's priorities, needs, and potential objections will determine the words you choose. For instance, think again about that reader with the loose dog. What is the most sensitive way to refer to his pet? Because the dog's behavior bothers you, you might be tempted to call him a *mutt*. But the derogatory meaning of that term will anger your reader. *Animal* is an alternative possibility, but it still sounds demeaning. *Dog* is the most neutral choice, but *pet* is perhaps the best word because it refers to the dog the way the owner probably thinks of him.

Here is a revision of the letter, one that carefully considers the reader:

Dear Neighbor,
I wanted to let you know that your pet has been running loose in the neighborhood when you're not home. As I'm sure you're aware, the

law requires that dogs be on leashes. I know you want your pet to be safe, but when he's running loose, he's in danger of being hit by a car or being picked up by animal control officers. If you'll give me a call, I'll tell you about some inexpensive products I've found that keep my pets in my yard.

This revised letter, which illustrates the specific things to do—and not do—to persuade a reader to accept your ideas, has a better chance than the first version of achieving its purpose.

> **TIP:**
>
> *Strive to produce papers and documents that are attractive and easy to read. Your decisions about font size and style, page layout, and paper quality will contribute to the appearance of your compositions. Don't ever send messy documents to your readers.*

Match Your Points to Your Reader

The most effective composition always matches the writer's ideas to the reader's priorities and needs. Therefore, the first way to compose with sensitivity is to include only those points, ideas, opinions, and arguments that are directly relevant to your reader. Let's say, for example, that you wish to convince a reader to spay or neuter her pet cats to help reduce the pet overpopulation problem. You could offer many reasons in support of your opinion, including:

1. Lower upkeep costs (fewer mouths to feed, fewer veterinary bills)
2. Less hassle (time and inconvenience required to care for and find homes for kittens)
3. Reduction in the number of animals euthanized at the local animal shelter
4. Lower license fees
5. Lower taxes
6. Health benefits for the cats

However, not all of these arguments will affect all readers. To select appropriate points to include, you'll need to think more about who your specific reader is. If she's a typical pet owner, she won't want to load herself with extra chores. She'll probably also have some emotional feelings for animals because she has pets. She's likely to care for her pets and to want them to live long, healthy lives. She's also likely to feel some compassion for homeless animals. Therefore, the most effective arguments for this reader are probably numbers 2, 3, and 6. You would not use these same arguments to a backyard breeder who sells kittens at the local flea market on weekends for extra cash. For that reader, you might want to offer reasons 1, 4, and 5, all of which focus on money, to help him realize that, ultimately, he's not making as much as he thinks he is.

For a second illustration, consider writing a memo to your supervisor to propose a change in a work procedure. To decide what points to present, first consider who the reader is. She's in a position of responsibility. She wants to make cost-effective decisions that will satisfy her customers. So, what arguments will convince her to make your proposed change? Use arguments that point out how your proposal will save the company money, generate more business, or deliver your product or service faster or more efficiently to the customer. She is less likely to be swayed by arguments that focus on benefits to her employees, unless you show her how these benefits will lead to increased productivity, profits, and happier customers, her three main priorities. It's not that you shouldn't mention the lighter workload and reduced stress that the change will bring to you and your co-workers. You just want to place more emphasis on the points that match your reader's major goals.

When matching points to a specific reader, it's a good idea to consider whether or not that particular individual will be most affected by logical arguments, emotional arguments, or a combination of the two. Logical arguments are based on hard facts and empirical evidence. For example, if you want to convince your reader to buy a certain brand of paper towels, you could explain how that brand's physical makeup results in greater absorbency, or how it's more cost-effective than other brands because you get more towels for less money. These are the logical arguments that support your recommendation. In addition, you can also add emotional arguments to your appeal. If your reader has children, for example, you can argue (as many television commercials do) that buying this specific brand makes him a better parent because the quick, easy cleanup will prevent him from getting upset about messes his kids make. Emotional arguments target a reader's needs for love, friends, fun, power, and influence. As you're deciding on the most appropriate points to include, categorize each one as either logical or emotional to help you tailor specific arguments to specific readers.

EXERCISE 11.1　*Matching Points to Reader*

Which of the arguments in each list are best suited to the different readers?

Thesis: You should add regular swimming to your fitness regimen.

Reasons:
a.　Improved cardiovascular health
b.　Improved physical appearance (weight loss, muscle tone)
c.　Expanded social life
d.　Economical activity
e.　Increased endurance and flexibility for other sports
f.　Family-oriented activity

1.　A group of senior citizens
2.　A single mother
3.　A teenager involved in high school athletics

Thesis: The City Council should purchase a historic house in the downtown district and make it into a museum.

Reasons:
a.　Preservation of local history and architecture
b.　Symbolic of the citizens' pride in their heritage
c.　Increased revenue for city
d.　Increased tourism
e.　More jobs in downtown area

4.　The owner of a business in the downtown area
5.　A member of the city council
6.　Readers of the city's local newspaper

TIP:

Carefully evaluate each one of your logical arguments to make sure you're not guilty of faulty reasoning. Some common pitfalls include overgeneralization, oversimplified cause/effect relationships, and inaccurate analogies.

Make Concessions

We don't write for readers who already know the information we're presenting or who already agree with our viewpoint. Doing so would be "preaching to the choir," a waste of time and effort. Because we write, then, to inform our readers or to convince them to believe what we believe, we can assume one of two things about them: (1) they haven't yet made up their minds or formulated their own opinions about the topic; or (2) they support the opposing viewpoint, which is why we need to write to persuade them to change their minds. In either case, our readers are likely to have at least a few preconceived ideas and opinions about the topic before they begin reading.

Keeping this in mind, you can write more successful compositions if you offer your readers **concessions,** or acknowledgments of their preexisting opinions, disagreements, and objections. Obviously, you have to consider your reader carefully to include appropriate concessions. Just as you match your points to your reader's goals and priorities, you must match your concessions to your reader's most likely objections. You have to anticipate her arguments and, as you write, acknowledge that they exist. For instance, if you were to write that essay urging the reader to spay or neuter her pet cats, you would acknowledge her specific concerns about this suggestion. She is likely to resist the idea because of the cost of the procedure. She may also object because of her fear that the operation will alter her pets' personalities. In your essay, you would want to mention these concerns.

Right now as you read this chapter, for example, you may be objecting to the whole notion of concessions. You might be thinking of two potential dangers that will weaken your composition. First, you might object to concessions based on your concern that they will serve only to remind the reader of the opposing arguments, thus reinforcing them in his mind. Second, you may be inclined to reject the suggestion that you include concessions because you fear you'll only mention arguments that the reader hasn't even considered, thus adding even more support for the opposing viewpoint. While these potential dangers do exist, the advantages of concessions almost always outweigh the disadvantages.

Including concessions will actually strengthen your composition in three specific ways. First, they demonstrate your understanding of the whole issue, not just one side. As a result, the reader will judge you to be a more credible source of information and more willingly accept your ideas. Second, they help you establish your good will toward the reader by acknowledging his viewpoint. Offering a concession is the written equivalent of *listening* to the other person, giving him a chance to have his say. As a result, he will be more likely to consider your views because he feels you are sensitive to his opinion. Finally, concessions are valuable because they allow the writer to respond to and refute specific objections to his ideas. After acknowledging a particular concern or disagreement, the writer can very thoroughly present all of the evidence that argues against it. This will help the reader understand how each of his particular concerns might be addressed.

To understand the effects of omitting concessions, read the following student's letter to her senator:

Homelessness in the United States has become a major problem. Thousands of Americans, many of whom are mentally ill, are wandering the streets with nowhere to go. Our government must do more for these unfortunate people.

First of all, the government can start by giving them alternatives to sleeping on the street. Build more temporary shelters and more low-cost housing for the homeless.

Secondly, after the government has helped these people get off the streets, it should find them jobs. New government programs could provide education and on-the-job training. For those unable to do physical labor, the government should find sedentary jobs that aren't very strenuous. For example, they could work as secretaries or something like that. Or they could work with children or the elderly.

In conclusion, the government must do a little more to solve this major problem. We have to take care of those who need help.

One quick reading of this letter reveals the writer's total lack of consideration for her reader. The senator who received this letter undoubtedly had some valid objections to these proposals. For instance, what about money? How would "the government" pay for all of these shelters and housing? Wouldn't a tax increase be necessary? Wouldn't his constituents object to such an increase? Where would "the government" get the resources (money, materials, and manpower) for the new programs the writer proposes? Finally, how many "sedentary" jobs are there to go around? (And since when is working with children or the elderly sedentary?)

The lack of concessions in this letter shows that the writer really doesn't understand the whole issue. Also, because the writer makes no effort to overcome the reader's concerns and disagreements, the senator probably did not seriously consider her proposals.

If you still fear that concessions will undermine your arguments, make sure you adhere to the following guidelines to reduce the potential dangers:

Keep concessions brief. Mention the argument or objection, but don't elaborate. The more detail you include, the greater the chance that you might reinforce or augment the reader's opposition. Usually, a brief one-sentence statement will sufficiently acknowledge the argument. Then, move on immediately to refute it with your own evidence and explanations.

Don't end with concessions. Concessions are more effective when you present them at the beginnings of your paragraphs and then go on to prove them invalid with your own ideas and evidence. When you end a paragraph with a concession, you're leaving the reader with that contrary thought rather than your viewpoint. Match the concessions you need to make to each of your points, and then thoroughly refute each one with a fully developed paragraph (see Chapters 4 and 5). Whatever you do, don't save all of your concessions for the end of your composition; the reader will finish it thinking of the opposing viewpoint rather than your own.

Signal the beginning and end of a concession. Certain transition words signal to the reader when a concession begins and ends. Common words and phrases used to introduce a concession include:

Admittedly,	It's true that
Granted,	Yes,

Of course,   I agree that
I concede that   I understand that

Follow your concession with another clear transition to signal that you will now refute that point. These transitions include words such as *However, But,* and *On the contrary.*

The following passages provide effective examples of concessions (in bold print). Transition words are italicized:

I've heard lots of people say that the decisions made by the Council are cut and dried and made long before the Council ever meets. *Actually* that doesn't happen as often as you might think. None of us on the City Council claims to have all the answers. **Yes, the members of the Council may have given a topic a lot of thought before they come to the meetings,** *but* if you attend and ask questions or voice your opinion you may have a new slant on an issue that hasn't occurred to anyone else.[1]

. . . [Social Security trust funds] do indeed exist. They're invested in special Treasury bonds, earning an average of 7.75 percent in 1997. **Yes, the government spends the money**—just as it spends any money that you, personally, invest in Treasury securities. *But* you know that you'll get your money back when your Treasuries mature, and Social Security will, too. If there's not enough money on hand, the government will borrow to cover the debt. Medicare has been redeeming Treasuries from its trust fund for the past three years.[2]

Bryce is correct that the orange traffic cones are ugly and that the shallow end [of the pool] is slippery. If he wants to get bent out of shape over these relatively minor inconveniences, then he should look at the foot-dragging of the Parks staff or go swim somewhere else rather than attacking environmentalists or the [endangered species] listing of the salamander.[3]

I realize that children care about their physical appearance. They don't want to look different from their friends. *However,* if all parents require their children to wear bicycle helmets, they will all look alike.

TIP:

To fully understand the opposing viewpoint, debate your topic with someone who disagrees with your thesis. Your opponent's arguments will help you know what concessions to include in your composition.

EXERCISE 11.2   *Concessions*

Add possible concessions that match each of the points in the following outlines:

I. Thesis: No college course should be required for a degree; a student should create an individual program of study by selecting courses he or she wants to take.

    A. Students should not be forced to take courses that are too difficult or beyond their intellectual abilities.

       Concession: _____

    B. Students should not be forced to take courses in subjects they won't need for their careers.

       Concession: _____

    C. College is too expensive to force a student to take courses in subjects he or she doesn't want to take.

       Concession: _____

    D. Students would enjoy their educations more if they took only classes they found interesting.

       Concession: _____

II. Thesis: The United States Congress should pass a law that permits a senator or representative to serve no more than two terms in office.

    A. The writers of the Constitution did not intend for political office to become a career.

       Concession: _____

    B. A career politician tends to focus on what he should do to get reelected rather than on what's best for the country.

       Concession: _____

    C. Absolute power corrupts absolutely.

        Concession: _____

    D. A more frequent turnover of government servants would allow more citizens to directly participate in the governing of our country.

        Concession: _____

    E. A more frequent turnover would encourage the exchange of new ideas.

        Concession: _____

Avoid Offending or Insulting Your Reader

Can you remember the last time someone insulted either you personally or a group with which you were affiliated? Your first reaction was probably to become defensive, maybe even angry. Your next reaction was probably to completely reject all of the ideas and opinions of the person who insulted you. Readers experience the same reaction when they are offended by a composition. As writers, then, we must take care to avoid insensitive language, for no matter how brilliant our ideas, an insulted reader will dismiss them outright. Thus, the composition will not fulfill its purpose.

This section presents three specific types of insensitive language—name-calling, statements that create a condescending or dismissive tone, and emotionally loaded terms—that will threaten the success of your composition.

Name-calling

The first type of insensitive language is **name-calling,** or using derogatory labels to describe people or groups. Writers use this technique in an attempt to cast doubt upon or to destroy the credibility of an opponent's ideas by personally attacking that individual or his character. In reality, though, this most blatantly insensitive tactic usually produces the reverse effect. Name-calling only brands the *writer* as immature, petty, and hostile.

For example, one magazine article repeatedly refers to Democrats as "Dumbocrats."[4] In a letter to a newspaper editor, a high school student who disagrees with the viewpoint of the cheerleading squad refers to them as "dumb bunnies," "rah rahs," and "silly pom pom shakers." Not only does he repeatedly denigrate the cheerleaders, but also, by extension, all female readers of his letter. Not surprisingly, both of these writers sound like mean, overemotional children, and the logical points they include are completely overshadowed by their insults.

Here are a few more examples of name-calling:

The Confederate flag is a religious symbol rather than the symbol of racism that *some ludicrous cults* claim.

John Roth is the type of *intellectual charlatan* who wants to use the Holocaust as a weapon to score really cheap political points.[5]

When I received my first issue of *The American Spectator,* I thought it bore an uncanny resemblance to *Mad* magazine. There was the same *juvenile* sense of satire and the same *pre-adolescent "girls are icky" attitude.* I don't think *you boys* have grown up much since then.

Adult women don't want to get their news from the perspective of an *immature, pre-adolescent boy.* Your news articles are terribly two-dimensional, verging on a simplistic black-and-white view of the world. Although full of facts, your articles make no distinctions between important facts and unimportant ones. It's as if *your authors lack the real life experiences* necessary to evaluate events in terms of their relative significance.[6]

You cannot build up yourself or your ideas by tearing down someone else. You will only damage your own credibility when you resort to childish attacks upon others. So focus on exposing the flaws in *ideas,* not in the people who believe them.

Finally, don't forget that the intelligent reader will "read between the lines" to discern *implied* insults, as well. For example, a newsmagazine published the following brief article:

Taking a timeout doesn't seem to be enough for the 70 percent of Americans who say spanking children is OK—despite a report by the American Academy of Pediatrics. Corporal punishment's popular among folks in small towns. But among educated city dwellers, it gets a bum rap.[7]

Although this passage includes no direct name-calling, one alert reader took offense, as he explains in his letter to the editor:

In five lines of text, you manage to insult not only the 70 percent of Americans who approve of spanking children but millions of us who are not "educated city dwellers." What makes you think that education is more prevalent in the city than in the country?[8]

This reader perceived the implication that "folks" who live in small towns are uneducated and, therefore, backward in their attitude about corporal punishment.

Condescending or Dismissive Tone

The second type of insensitive language includes statements that state or imply the reader or her idea is ignorant, uninformed, illogical, or wrong. Such statements produce an arrogant, condescending tone of "talking down" to the reader, suggesting that she is inferior. A writer will not convert a reader to his opinions by implying that the reader is stupid. The following statements include examples of insensitive phrases:

Do you ever wonder what happens inside an ambulance? Do you believe paramedics simply move sick and injured people from one place to another? *Well, think again!*

Sheriff Sherwood, *you need to grow up. If you were the kind of man you should be,* the community would support your decisions.

The apartment I want is just around the corner, so you may think it wouldn't make sense for me to move there. *If you do, then you're completely missing the point.*

I hope you understand my directions. However, *if you do have trouble figuring them out*, call me at my office.

Avoid any suggestion that the reader is mentally deficient or unenlightened.

TIP:

For more about tone, see Chapter 8.

Emotionally Loaded Words

Chapter 10 discussed the denotative (dictionary) and connotative (emotional) meanings of words. The connotative meanings of words help us accurately and confidently communicate our thoughts and feelings about a topic. They also help us urge the reader to feel a certain way about that topic. If you use the word *inexpensive* to describe a couch, you are suggesting to the reader that the buyer found a good deal. If you describe the same couch as *cheap,* you suggest not only that its price is low, but also that its quality is poor. Some readers will even attach the extra meanings of "tawdry" or "shoddy" to that particular adjective. Also, compare the words *assertive* and *aggressive.* Favorable connotations are attached to the former, while the unfavorable suggestions of "pushy" and "overbearing" are attached to the latter.

For another example, look at the following sentence, which comes from an essay claiming that the late rock-and-roll singer Elvis Presley "has come to symbolize pure and absolute corruption":

Elvis was *fat, half-dead, bloated* and *sweating,* tossing soaked scarves into the audience, *walking through cruel parodies* of his songs.[9]

This statement is obviously very harsh because of the emotionally loaded words, which the writer chose to encourage the reader to form a negative reaction to his subject. These words are indeed forceful and assertive. However, words like *fat, bloated,* and *sweating* are clearly derogatory and insulting. An Elvis fan reading this sentence would become defensive, even angry; therefore, the essay would not convince her to change her mind.

Assertive word choices must be tempered by a consideration of the reader's feelings. Using language that is bold but offensive will cause the reader to reject your ideas. Often, we need to tone down a statement by choosing words more sensitive to that reader. For example, you might revise the sentence above as follows:

Elvis was overweight, tired, perspiring, tossing soaked scarves into the audience, singing his songs without feeling.

Though this revision obviously is much less forceful, it is much more sensitive to the reader who may happen to like Elvis and his music.

Another example of emotionally loaded language comes from an animal activist publication. In an article about "liberators" who buy lobsters from supermarkets and then release them into the ocean, the author uses very emotional words and phrases:

Once the lobsters were *sprung* from their grocery store *gloom,* the *rescue team* . . . carefully packed the shellfish in coolers according to plan: first "blue ice" packs were placed on the bottom, followed by wet newspapers, then the lobsters were placed on top covered by more wet newspaper. After an hour-and-a-half drive, the lobsters and their *support crew* arrived at the release site, a semi-secluded beach in New Hampshire. Although the lobsters seemed "lively and ready to go," said [Richard] Griffin, they were first placed in shallow water so they could adjust to their new environment and the *activists* could remove the rubber bands binding their claws. Now, *free from bondage,* the crustaceans were led (or rather, *gently carried*) to the *promised* water, to *freedom,* to their *home* in the Atlantic.[10]

The writer uses this kind of language intentionally to stir the reader's sympathy for the lobsters.

On a final note, remember that all vulgar, sexist, and racist language is also emotionally loaded and offensive. Do not include curse words, gender-related insults, or racial slurs in your writing.

TIP:

> For more about the connotative meanings of words, see Chapter 10.

EXERCISE 11.3 *Sensitive Language*

Rewrite the following sentences to increase their sensitivity to the reader:

1. Smokers damage their own bodies and then annoy us nonsmokers with their stupidity and selfishness.

2. Some retired people are housebound because of health problems, but most retired people are just too lazy to go out and find something to do.

3. Police officers risk their lives every day. They do it for rude, ungrateful people like you, people who insult and disrespect them.

4. There is more than one generation of misfit parents out there who are suckers for anti-[corporal] punishment baloney.[11]

5. If I were stupid enough to pay $400 for a pair of shoes, I certainly would not admit it.

6. Television viewers are sick of media vultures who exploit victims of violence to get high ratings.

7. Now, there are two guilty parties responsible for [misuse of lawsuits]: 1. The lawyers who have peddled this abominable corruption upon us out of their own selfish interests; and 2. The public, who out of stupidity and greed allow it to happen and who as juries create the ridiculous judgments that have brought such nauseous feelings to all sensible members of society.[12]

8. The Americans with Disabilities Act passed by Congress is another sample of never-ending special interest legislative garbage. It was no doubt slathered with a generous dose of do-goodism as well as sincere, although misguided, goodwill.[13]

9. People . . . remain callously oblivious to the sad fact that rampant animal overpopulation makes it agonizingly necessary to abort thousands of helpless puppies and kittens, simply because there are not enough good homes for all of them and because thoughtless people do not have their animals sterilized.[14]

10. Wimpy environmentalists are crying big fat tears because a bunch of headhunters in Brazil are chopping down some trees to make a little extra spending money. These fruitcake Chicken Littles believe if we chop up jungles there won't be any more air and we'll all die. Hogwash! They can PAVE the darn rain forests for all I care.[15]

Chapter Summary

If you want your composition to convince the reader to accept your idea or opinion, you will have to write with sensitivity to that reader. **Match your points** to your reader's major goals and priorities, and **offer concessions** to acknowledge his potential objections. To avoid offending or insulting him, **refrain from name-calling, condescending statements,** and **emotionally loaded language.**

Suggested Writing Activities

As you write one or more of the following compositions, remember the techniques for composing with sensitivity and tact.

1. Write a letter to your senator or congressional representative to propose a needed change to your state or region.

2. Argue to a friend or relative that he or she should begin a fitness program.

3. Argue that something is a waste of money.

4. Argue in support of a particular charity or nonprofit organization.

5. Write a rebuttal to an editorial you disagree with.

6. Write a letter to a professor requesting an extension on an assignment's due date.

7. Write a memo to your company president requesting a specific benefit (e.g., longer vacation, a 401K plan, flextime, etc.).

Notes

1. Mel Cohen, "City Council Seeks Your Opinions," *The News Herald*, Morganton, N.C. (May 3, 1998), 4A.

2. Jane Bryant Quinn, "What Price Reform?" *Newsweek* (June 22, 1998), 57.

3. Bill Bunch, "Postmarks," *The Austin Chronicle* (June 19–25, 1998), www.auschron.com/current/cols.postmarks.html, 1.

4. William Tucker, "Byting the Hand That Feeds Us," *American Spectator* (May 1998), 24ff.

5. John Podhoretz, "Waxing Roth: Holocaust Museum Follies Part II," *The New York Post* (June 19, 1998), www.nypostonline.com/commentary/3523.html, 1.

6. Carole Siemens, "Correspondence," *American Spectator* (October 1998), 89.

7. "New Report: Don't Slap Me, Silly," *Newsweek* (April 20, 1998), 6.

8. Gordon Molesworth, "Letters," *Newsweek* (May 11, 1998), 20. Reprinted by permission of the author.

9. Steve Hammer, "Elvis Presley and the Society of Hate," *NUVO Newsweekly* (January 12, 1994), www.nuvo.net/hammer/hamelvis/html, 1.

10. Kirsten Rosenberg, "Homeward Bound," *The Animals' Agenda* (September/October 1998), 39.

11. "Anti-Punishment Frenzy," *WhatWhat* (1997), www.whatwhat.com/comment/hit_kid.html, 1.

12. "Lawsuits—Tyranny of the Ridiculous," *WhatWhat* (1996), www.whatwhat.com/comment/legal1.html, 1.

13. "New Privileged Class," *WhatWhat* (1997), www.whatwhat.com/comment/privileg.html, 1.

14. Donna Worthington, "Letters," *The Animals' Agenda* (September/October 1998), 5.

15. Ed Anger, "Pave the Stupid Rain Forests!" quoted in Daniel McDonald and Larry W. Burton, *The Language of Argument* (New York: HarperCollins, 1996), 113.

Appendix   Sample Student Compositions

The following composition is a narrative that successfully uses vivid language. Notice how the writer uses factual and sensory details, descriptive adjectives, action verbs, and figurative language to recreate his experience for the reader.

A Time I Did Something Crazy

While stationed in the Army at West Point, New York, I met Scott Owens, a thin, lanky man from Wisconsin. Scott got me interested in rappelling, took me under his wing, and taught me the basics of this thrilling sport. As I became more familiar with basic technique, he introduced me to Australian descent rappelling, the act of running face-first down a cliff or tower. Rappelling alone is a detailed and meticulous sport requiring concentration and attention to detail. One wrong knot or false step can hurl the rappeller to the earth, resulting in grave injury or death. I finally gained enough confidence in "Aussie style" to try "free-fall Aussie," where the rappeller purposely falls toward the ground with no foot support.

Once I ensured that I was properly harnessed and "tied in," making sure the rope was properly set, I slowly leaned out over the vast expanse of Fort Dix, New Jersey, forty feet up with only my feet touching a horizontal metal beam affixed to the open side of the rappel tower. My right hand tightened across my chest, holding the half-inch rope taut in leather gloves. Below, I could see the ocean of sand that was to be my destination. Slowly, I leaned further out until my body was horizontal, face-down and scared to death. Scott tried to relax me by giving words of assurance and comfort, much the way any parent would try to soothe a child who caught a glimpse of Freddie Krueger on late-night TV.

Finally, I got up enough nerve and pushed away forcefully with my feet from the tower, simultaneously stretching my right arm out to my side, releasing my brake. I heard the constant zip of the rope through my glove and felt the heat created by the friction of the rope rushing through my hand. The air blasted my face, and the ocean of sand rose up to meet me. In two seconds, I had fallen thirty feet. I quickly reached my right arm back across my chest to apply the brakes. I came to a nearly sudden stop only eight feet above the ground. I could pick out sand grains and small pebbles not visible from the top of the tower. I slowly lowered myself to the ground. There, I decided that one trip was all I needed.

The following is an excerpt from a professional report about elevators and handicapped accessibility. It includes vivid language such as strong verbs and precise word choices.

All elevators must measure a minimum of 60 inches by 60 inches. Handicapped accessible elevators in buildings of three stories or less must measure 68 inches wide by 51 inches deep. Also, they must support a minimum capacity of 2,000 pounds. One elevator in our building falls below the standards of interior size and maneuverability.

To reach this elevator, a handicapped individual entering from outside must pass through four sets of double doorways. Two of these doorways open automatically. The other two open with a push bar in the middle of the door. Once an individual is through all of these doors, he must turn his wheelchair 90 degrees into the hallway where the elevator is located. This hallway measures 3 feet 4 inches wide. After executing a 90-degree turn into this narrow passage, the individual must then turn another 90 degrees to enter the elevator cab. He must squeeze through a door space that measures only 2 feet 10 inches. Once through the door, he will find himself in a tiny, cramped space measuring only 51 inches by 57 inches. Obviously, a physically challenged individual must struggle to gain access to this particular elevator.

The next composition is a summary of a film entitled Mary Reilly. *It includes effective vivid language.*

A Summary of *Mary Reilly*

Mary Reilly serves as a maid in Dr. Jekyll's gloomy mansion. Every evening, he disappears into his laboratory alone, and Mary often wakes to the sound of screams and other strange noises. Despite his mysterious behavior, Mary becomes fond of her kind master, who encourages her to confide in him about her abusive past.

One day, Dr. Jekyll announces to his household staff that he has hired an assistant named Mr. Hyde. Afterward, the staff catches only glimpses of an elusive, limping figure. While she's tidying the doctor's study one evening, the repulsive Mr. Hyde suddenly appears, gropes her, and startles her with his knowledge of her past.

Meanwhile, Mary's affection for Dr. Jekyll grows, and he begins asking her to complete strange errands for him, such as accompanying Mr. Hyde to the market to purchase butchered animal organs. Hyde, outspoken and offensive, abruptly reveals to Mary Dr. Jekyll's desire for her.

Mr. Hyde becomes increasingly violent. He murders several people, one of them a prominent acquaintance of Dr. Jekyll's, and is forced to flee. Mary, returning from her mother's funeral, encounters him on the street, where he kisses her passionately. Back at the mansion, the police question her about Mr. Hyde's whereabouts, and she lies to protect him. She learns that the pain-racked Dr. Jekyll, too, is protecting Mr. Hyde.

Mr. Hyde suddenly reappears one morning in the doctor's bedroom. Mary tries to run away, but he grabs her. He tells her Dr. Jekyll concocted a potion that transforms him into the evil Hyde. The doctor also created a second potion that turns him back into himself, but Hyde reveals that he has gained the power to emerge from Jekyll at will.

Mary decides to leave the mansion and packs her belongings. But she can't resist another peek into the doctor's laboratory. There, Hyde grabs her and kisses her violently. He holds a knife to her throat, but she doesn't flinch. When she reaches up to caress his cheek, his murderous impulse fades. Mr. Hyde injects himself with a potion and begins to howl and convulse with pain. As Mary watches in horror, a crying baby rises up out of Hyde's chest, struggling to break free. Hyde and the being within him wrestle in agony for a few moments, then Hyde suddenly transforms into Jekyll again. Dr. Jekyll manages to tell Mary that Mr. Hyde added poison to the potion, then he dies in her arms.

This composition is a professional report about the impact of development on wildlife. It demonstrates clear organization and effective layers of development.

Reduction of Negative Environmental Impact on Wildlife at the Project Site

Overview

As we proceed with plans for our project to build a dock and a gazebo around the pond, we should bear in mind that numerous changes to the environment might adversely impact the wildlife on the site. This report will present ways we can minimize negative consequences to wildlife that could result from construction. Proper management of the natural resources includes protection of open water sources and vegetation, in addition to enhancing wildlife habitation by adding helpful structures.

Protection of Open Water Sources

To protect the water in the creek and pond, we will need to use the proper paving material. Asphalt contains an oily tar substance that, over time, may seep into the ground and, eventually, the water. The oily substance would spread a film over the water that could create problems for the wildlife community. For example, insects cannot lay their eggs in water that contains this oily element. A reduction in insect population may result in a reduction in the food supply for other life forms such as amphibians and crustaceans, which eat insect larvae. Furthermore, this oily substance may contaminate the drinking water for mice, squirrels, reptiles, rabbits, and birds. Concrete, however, does not contain this greasy element and can be used without risk of runoff or seepage contamination to open water sources. Therefore, concrete is the preferred paving material.

Vegetation

As recommended by the Wildlife Resources Agency, vegetation should be maintained in a layered or vertical structure. As illustrated in Figure 1, a healthy vertical structure includes the herbaceous layer, shrub layer, and tree canopy. The shorter herbaceous layer, which is composed of

Tree Canopy

Shrub Layer

Herbaceous Layer

FIGURE 1 Vertical structure (From the Tennessee Game and Fish Commission)

grass and small plants, meets a diversity of needs for many animals. Some may eat, breed, or seek cover in this layer. The middle shrub layer consists of bushes, brush, vines, snags, etc. These may contain food berries or nuts and/or provide nesting and cover sites for animals such as rabbits. The tallest layer, the tree canopy, provides dens, nests, roosts, perches, and hard and soft mast foods for animals such as squirrels and birds. This layered or vertical structure of vegetation provides seasonal diversity of food, which is critical to the survival of many wildlife species.

Clearly, all forms of vegetation are useful to wildlife. As we begin construction on the project site, we must maintain successive stages of vegetation to attract and support a greater variety of wildlife. In addition, we should keep these stages close together to allow for safe travel by animals between areas.

Special vegetation concerns for this project include the snags commonly found in the shrub layer. Snags, which occur naturally, are dead logs and stumps, either standing or downed. Some snags in the forest appear dangerously close to falling or have already fallen across the nature trail areas. However unsightly, this form of decaying vegetation is used by small rodents and other animals, such as cottontail rabbits, for nests, shelter, and winter dens. Removal of all snags can greatly reduce the various wildlife species and populations on the project site. One desirable alternative involves moving them further into the woods whenever possible.

Helpful Structures

Adding certain types of structures would enhance or attract wildlife habitation in the project area. These additions may increase the enjoyment of those who use the nature trails or pond, as well as provide other benefits such as the natural control of some insect populations. Bats, for instance, are natural predators of mosquitoes and other pests. Providing bat houses for them would help reduce the mosquito population. Construction of squirrel nest boxes on some of the trees in the forest may encourage increased habitation for these animals. As illustrated in Figure 2, squirrel nest boxes are made from a rough lumber exterior with cloth-lined floors and hinged tops. They are mounted on trees at about twenty feet off the ground.

Many people enjoy observing birds. The addition of birdhouses and feeders in the area may attract increased numbers and varieties of birds. These structures, which also aid birds in finding suitable perches, nests,

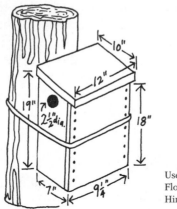

Use 1″ rough lumber.
Floor—1/2″ hardware cloth.
Hinge top so box can be cleaned.

FIGURE 2   Squirrel nest box (From the Tennessee Game and Fish Commission)

and feeding sites, may range in design from simple gourds to more elaborate, decorative feeders and houses.

Conclusion

Although some changes in the natural environment will be necessary to complete our project, utilization of these resource management ideas will reduce potential harm to the wildlife community. Protection of water and vegetation and the addition of helpful structures are simple suggestions that can benefit wildlife and aid in the successful completion of this project.

The following composition is an essay about an alternative rock musician. It includes effective layers of development and vivid language.

Kurt Cobain's Contributions to Music

"Rarely since the Beatles had rock undergone such a creative convulsion. Cobain and his band Nirvana appropriated the frenzies of so-called alternative music and transformed them into mainstream mania," proclaimed *Rolling Stone* magazine. "Kurt Cobain's telling insights and uncompromising attitude made him one of rock's most admired stars." As lead singer, lyricist, and lead guitarist of the band Nirvana, Cobain helped ignite a new rock revolution in the music industry. By way of his compassion and personal beliefs, Cobain also stimulated awareness of critical issues through his music. Kurt Cobain made everlasting contributions to the world of music as well as to society. As a result, when he died in 1994 at the age of twenty-seven, Cobain left this world as one of music's most influential artists.

With Kurt Cobain as the artistic force behind the band, Nirvana launched the explosion of alternative rock music into the mainstream music scene. The monumental event that initiated this music revolution happened during the summer of 1992. Nirvana's *Nevermind* album soared out of the blue to knock out and replace Michael Jackson's *Dangerous* album as the number one selling album on *Billboard's* Top 200 Albums chart. At the same time, Nirvana's teen angst-filled single "Smells Like Teen Spirit" edged its way into the top five on *Billboard's* Top 100 Singles chart. *Nevermind* went on to sell over five million copies in the United States and over nine million copies worldwide. Nirvana's success and critical acclaim continued to surge after the multiplatinum selling *Nevermind* album. For instance, Nirvana won Best New Artist at both the 1992 MTV Music Awards and the 1993 American Music Awards. Then, in the fall of 1993, Nirvana accomplished a very unique feat when their *In Utero* album debuted at the number one position on *Billboard's* Top 200 Albums, selling over 200,000 copies in its first week of release. Again in the fall of 1994, Nirvana's *Nirvana Unplugged in New York* album debuted at the number one position on *Billboard's* Top 200 Albums, selling over 400,000 copies in its first week of release. Nirvana continued to receive critical recognition for its music as *Nirvana Unplugged in New York* won for Best Alternative Rock Album at the 1995 American Music Awards. Nirvana's admiration from music critics as well as music listeners opened the door for other alternative rock bands to succeed in the mainstream music scene. Bands such as Pearl Jam, Stone Temple Pilots, the Smashing Pumpkins, and Bush all gained new-found fame as well as persevering success. These bands combined have sold over forty million albums in the United States alone from 1992 to 1997.

Above all of these achievements, none meant more to Kurt Cobain than the gratification of being able to address significant social issues. Long known as a women's rights activist, Cobain continually stressed in his songs issues such as rape, apathy, and the inequality of women. Songs consciously aware of rape and violence against women include "Polly," "Negative Creep," and "Rape Me." . . . In a monologue on Nirvana's 1992 *Incesticide* album cover, Cobain speaks about his wife,

Courtney Love: "My wife challenges injustice, and the reason her character has been so severely attacked is because she chooses not to function the way the white corporate man insists." He goes on to make a request of Nirvana fans: "If any of you in any way hate homosexuals, people of different color, or women, please do this one favor for us— leave us . . . alone! Don't come to our shows and don't buy our records." Nirvana performed at numerous benefit concerts to raise both awareness and funds for rape victim support groups. Nirvana also performed at various pro-choice benefit concerts, in addition to contributing songs to benefit albums such as *No Alternative,* which helped raise money for AIDS research.

Kurt Cobain's many triumphs and important contributions left a lasting legacy. His musical creativity changed the face of mainstream music. Also, his compassionate emphasis on social issues helped more than a few people. We can only speculate about the many more positive contributions he could have made had he not died so young.

This next composition is a literary analysis essay that analyzes the plot of a particular short story. It contains a strong opening, clear organization, effective layers of development, and a good closing.

The Old South and the New South in Faulkner's "A Rose for Emily"

William Faulkner's short story "A Rose for Emily" is a tale about a murder in a small Southern town. One of the town's most revered residents, Miss Emily Grierson, poisons her boyfriend when he refuses to make a long-term commitment to her. However, we readers don't discover that there's been a murder until the very last sentence of the story. Though we're offered many clues about what happened, we don't understand their relevance until the very end, when we're startled to suddenly realize that the reclusive, eccentric spinster not only killed her lover, but also slept beside his rotting corpse for many years. We don't understand these clues because Faulkner presents them to us in a mixed-up order. His nonchronological account of specific incidents in the plot produces several intriguing effects. The scrambled order of events not only results in a shocking surprise ending, but the form of the story also echoes its content: the narration of isolated, seemingly unconnected events reflects the method of acquiring information in a small town and also illustrates the struggle between the "old South" and the "new South."

First, Faulkner uses a scrambled order of events as a plot device to produce his surprise ending. He tells us about the bad smell emanating from Emily's house *before* he even introduces us to her lover, Homer Barron. Then we learn that she buys rat poison and, after that, a man's toilet set engraved with the letters H.B. Next, we find out about Homer's disappearance. It's almost impossible for the reader to discern the cause and effect relationship between these incidents because they are not related in chronological order. Consequently, when Faulkner provides the final description of Homer's rotten corpse in Emily's bed, all of the pieces of the puzzle instantly rearrange themselves in the reader's mind and click into place, producing a sudden, startling awareness of exactly what happened.

Furthermore, the scrambled order of events demonstrates Faulkner's use of the form of his story to reflect its content. The nonchronological plot order suggests the way information travels in a small town, where gossip is passed along in bits and pieces, resulting in incomplete understanding. The narrator of this tale obtains the details he relates from a variety of different sources. He learns of the foul smell from the mayor, who found out about it from one of Emily's neighbors and another unidentified man. The ladies of the town report her mental illness when her father dies. Many of the townspeople observe her riding around town in a carriage with Homer Barron. The druggist tells his story about her purchase of arsenic. The jeweler reveals her order of a man's toilet set. A group of townspeople, including the narrator, enter her bedroom after her death to finally discover her crime. Each of the residents of this small town has witnessed various details of Emily's life, but no one person knows *all* of the details. The narrator learns a little bit more from each person who sees or interacts with Emily, but like the reader, these fragments prevent any of them from making important connections. Thus, the small-town tradition of oral information exchange results in an incomplete picture of the truth until the last crucial detail is revealed.

Finally, Faulkner uses his scrambled plot to reflect the see-saw of emotions felt by the younger generation of the new South toward their ancestors of the old South. The narrator, who identifies himself as a representative of the more democratic-minded, younger generation, expresses feelings of pride, pity, and resentment toward Emily and her way of life. His vacillating emotions are apparent with each incident he relates. For example, his description of Emily's house displays his pride, but then her refusal to pay taxes provokes his resentment. He pities her when he learns of the foul smell, but reveals his resentment again when her father dies and people speculate that she'll finally know what it's like to be without money and therefore "humanized." For this narrator, Emily is a representative of the aristocratic old South era, and his feelings toward her reflect his various emotions toward his heritage. Like most Southerners, he feels pride in that heritage, but also feels angry toward those in the wealthiest classes who believed they were better than everyone else. Faulkner's fractured narration of events reflects these conflicting emotions of the younger generation toward their Southern ancestors.

So, Faulkner related the incidents of the story in a mixed-up order not only to surprise us at the end, but also to give us the same perspective as the townspeople. Clearly, Faulkner was not only a great storyteller, but also a master of his craft. His fictional technique reinforces his overall message about the tensions between the old South and the new South. Ultimately, Miss Emily wins the struggle between the generations by getting away with murder, but only because they let her. Though the new generation resents her, their respect and pity for her allow her to commit a heinous crime without punishment. Perhaps, then, Faulkner is pointing out the tendency of Southerners to tacitly accept even the worst aspects of their heritage.

The following composition is an essay urging parents to immunize their children. It successfully incorporates vivid language, an effective opening and closing, thorough layers of development, and concessions.

A Case for Immunizations

Tears flood a weary mother's troubled face as she holds an around-the-clock vigil at her sick son's bedside. Lying in a hospital bed, the child's body is as limp as a wilted flower's stem, and his skin is as pale as an eggshell. Only a few weeks ago, he was an active three-year-old who was constantly getting into harmless mischief. She truly longs for those wonderful days when she would catch him sneaking a snack from the cookie jar or pulling every toy from his toy box. His zest is now diminished. He is thoroughly exhausted from the continuous coughing and choking, and pneumonia has settled in his tiny lungs. He has been stricken with pertussis, otherwise known as the whooping cough. One thought keeps racing through his mother's troubled mind: "I could have prevented this horrible tragedy if I had only followed through on his immunizations."

Making sure that your young child receives all of his required immunizations on time can prevent the needless pain, suffering, and even death caused by a completely preventable disease. Like some parents, you might think that the immunizations are costly, time-consuming, and painful; however, you should consider the cost, time, and pain involved in contracting one of these terrible diseases.

Although immunizations can be expensive at a pediatrician's office, the county health department provides the same vaccines free of charge. However, cost does become a major issue when a child misses a scheduled vaccination, such as the hemophilus B injection, and then contracts the disease. *Hemophilus influenzae* type B can cause meningitis, pneumonia, and infections of other body systems such as blood, joints, bone, soft tissue under the skin and throat, and the covering of the heart. Imagine the tremendous cost of treating such a horrible disease. First of all, a lengthy hospital stay in a private room is inevitable. Then add the pediatrician's bill for daily visits, along with the cost of other physicians who provide treatment. Finally, the smaller charges for medicine and supplies will collect like dust. All of these fees can add up to an astronomical sum. Another cost consideration is the parents' lost wages while they remain at their ailing child's bedside.

Taking a child for immunizations can be time-consuming for a busy parent. Granted, getting away from work and picking up the child from daycare is a hassle, and the long wait at the health department can be frustrating. However, health department staff members often administer vaccines in groups and spread them far enough apart so that parents do not have to visit the health department every time they turn around. For example, the diphtheria, tetanus, and pertussis vaccine, known as the DTP, is given at two months, four months, six months, fifteen months, and between four and six years of age. The oral polio doses are given along with all of the DTPs, with the exception of the six-month dose. The hemophilus B and hepatitis B vaccines are also coordinated with the DTP visits. The measles, mumps, and rubella vaccination, known as the MMR, is given in conjunction with the fifteen-month and four-to-six years vaccinations. These five visits to the health department can prevent an extended absence from work to care for a sick child. Another consideration is the trouble you will have registering your child for kindergarten. The county schools will not enroll a child until she has received all required doses of each immunization. Because the shots must be complete before the beginning of the school year, the time available for bringing them up to date is limited.

It's understandable why many parents dread taking their children for immunizations. Hearing the small child's wails is enough to make a parent weep. However, the stinging pinpoint prick of a vaccine-filled needle cannot compare to the pain and suffering caused by even the mildest of the dreadful diseases. For example, the mumps causes fever, headache, and swollen glands under the jaw, and can also lead to hearing loss and even meningitis. As for the more severe diseases, such as polio, the symptoms are more relentless. Polio can cause severe muscle pain, difficult breathing, permanent paralysis, and, in the worst cases, death. Imagine the heartbreak of watching a child's small body deteriorate just like an elderly person's. These effects, some lifelong, are far more serious than a tiny needle prick that is over in a split second and easily forgotten after Mom's tender cuddles.

Considering all of the possible illnesses a child can contract by not receiving immunizations on time, parents need to make sure their children are vaccinated on schedule. Having your child immunized benefits both the child and the parents. The child's youthful days won't be interrupted by unnecessary ailments, and he or she can enjoy a healthy childhood. As for the parents, they won't endure worry or lost wages because of a devastating illness. Also, parents can rest assured that they've done their part to keep their children healthy.

The following letter to a newspaper's editor argues that public schools need nurses on staff. It includes effective supporting points and data to prove the author's point. It also exhibits sensitivity to the reader by offering concessions and using tactful language.

Do Our Schools Need Nurses?

Dear Editor:

Stanley, a red-headed second grader, came home from school crying. He told his mother he had gotten hurt at recess that morning, and his shoulder had been hurting him all day. A doctor discovered the second grader had broken his collarbone. This child had suffered all day without anyone recognizing the seriousness of his injury. Of course, he was only a child, and children get hurt, and everyone knows that children exaggerate their pain. Sadly, though, this second grader wasn't exaggerating. Could something similar happen again? The answer is yes, and the facts show it has already happened many times. How can we prevent a

child from getting hurt at school? Unfortunately, no matter what pre-
cautions we take, our children will get hurt at school. But we can cut
down on the severity of their injuries. How? By hiring a school nurse for
every school in Burke County.

Recently, county residents have been debating the issue of supplying
school nurses for Burke County schools. Many people, especially the
school system itself, parents, and the Burke County Health Department,
wholeheartedly support the hiring of school nurses. Having nurses at
schools makes perfect sense. I realize nurses cannot solve every medical
problem in our schools, but the identification of illnesses or injuries
would be more immediate. Maybe a little second grader wouldn't have
had to suffer or a mother wouldn't have had to doubt the safety of her
child while at school if a nurse had been there to help.

Some Burke County citizens object that there is not enough tax
money to pay for the hiring of nurses. They say that the money the county has set aside for the school system should be used for more important
school necessities. Like many others, I am also concerned how our county tax dollars are being spent. But the truth is very little of our local tax
money has been used to fund the school nurses program. For several
years, just two nurses serviced four middle schools and two high
schools. A Child Health Grant from the state of North Carolina has
always paid these nurses' salaries. Not one dollar of our local tax money
has ever gone to the two nurses. Recently, the success of an experimen-
tal nursing program at Hillcrest and Mountain View Elementary Schools
has led to the hiring of seven more school nurses who serve fifteen elementary schools. Burke County pays the salary of only one of these nurses. A Duke Endowment grant of $480,000 has been acquired to fund the
hiring of three of these nurses for three years while the Grace Healthcare
Foundation is raising $500,000 to pay for their salaries after the grant
money is spent. Grace Hospital, Valdese General Hospital, and the
Health Department Medicaid Fund Balance pay the salaries of the other
three nurses. This type of funding will continue to pay for school nurses
in the future. So, the spending of Burke County tax money has never
been and still is not an issue when it comes to placing nurses in our
schools.

It is also true our school system is not a health care provider. But one
nurse per school does not a health care provider make. Usually, we think
of a health care provider being a doctor, a group of doctors or special-
ists, or maybe an HMO. But never would we think of it as being one
nurse to hundreds of students. However, school nurses can provide

quick medical attention and prevent additional suffering until the parent can get the child to a physician.

It's also true that a school's main responsibility is the education of our children. But many employees of Burke County schools are not educators. A school needs many different noneducating staff to run smoothly. These staff members include cafeteria workers, custodians, secretaries, and maintenance crews. When we think about the jobs these employees do in our schools, we should see the issue of school nurses in a different light. Our noneducating personnel are necessary to the educating of our children. These necessary employees must now include school nurses.

Lastly, some argue that a responsible parent should not send an ill child to school. Most parents do not do this. They just want reasonable, competent health care for their children if the need arises. People who speak of irresponsible parents are also the people who believe that all a school nurse would be doing, if anything, is treating the cold, flu, and stomach aches. But that is only a minute portion of a school nurse's responsibility in one of our county schools. Following is a list of treatments and activities performed by the seven school nurses at the fifteen elementary schools in just the month of January 1999:

- 801 students were treated for colds, the flu, stomach illnesses, and injuries.
- 105 of the above students were referred to doctors.
- 84 screenings for vision, height, weight, and blood pressure were conducted.
- 625 screenings for head lice were done.
- 352 immunization records were reviewed to ensure they were up to date.
- 3,330 students received health education on such subjects as communicable diseases, personal hygiene, nutrition, exercise, and a healthy heart.
- Emergency action plans were formulated for health problems such as bee sting allergies, asthma, seizures, and heart conditions.
- 140 faculty members received training in the above emergency action plans.
- 225 parent conferences were held.
- 282 teacher conferences were held.

As adults, we demand prevention, precaution, and preparedness at our places of employment. Children in a Burke County school deserve the same right. They are the ones who will reap the immediate benefits of the school nurses program. These are also the same children who will grow up to be Burke County taxpayers. By that time, I feel certain that school nurses will be standard employees in the Burke County school system. These future taxpayers will willingly pay for nurses in their schools because they will want their children to have the best possible care, just as they had.

—Sandra E. Lail

This last composition is a memorandum written to argue that the company president should create a tuition reimbursement program for his employees. This writer successfully considers her reader by including appropriate arguments, concessions, and sensitive language.

To: Mr. Charles Morgan, President

From: Jean McMullin

Date: November 16, 1998

Re: New Benefit

I am proud to be a part of Bank of Burke. We do a great job providing solid service to our customers and our community. Your leadership and commitment to Total Quality Management empowers us to deliver solid service. Superior service is essential for the life of our bank and can only be achieved through continuous improvement, which along with employee involvement completes our TQM equation for creating customer satisfaction. As we strive to improve corporately and personally, I would like to recommend an employee tuition refund program as a means of continuous improvement. I realize this could be costly; however, a tuition refund program would be an investment in Bank of Burke's greatest asset . . . its employees.

As you weigh the costs and the benefits, I would like to suggest first the benefits to the bank. Offering employees a chance to further their education builds employee commitment and, therefore, lowers employee turnover. Training of new employees is costly to our bank in time and service. Employees want to believe you are interested in developing their job skills. A tuition refund program will help them develop new skills, which in turn leads to increased productivity, sales, and service.

Education and training also cultivate professionalism, which is so important in our industry. Another great benefit to the bank would be the development of a resource of trained employees for in-house advancements and future management candidates. Qualified candidates are scarce in today's labor market with our country's low unemployment rate, which is a critical reason for us to retain and develop our current employees.

Let's consider the tuition refund program as an employee benefit. You would be providing a means for self-development and self-realization, which, as I'm sure you are aware, is an important step in fulfilling employee needs. Education and training build job knowledge, confidence, and self-esteem. They also provide the employee opportunities for advancement and increased job satisfaction. Half of our current employees began their careers in banking as tellers. These employees, as well as new hires, would have an opportunity to advance and progress from teller to manager if they so desired.

Costs for this program could be shared with employees. I recommend we base our tuition refund on the grade the employee achieves. An A would be worth a 100 percent refund; a B, 90 percent; a C, 70 percent; a D or below would earn no refund. Employees would be responsible for books and study time. This would require a commitment from the employee. Class time and study time would be in the evenings after work. Currently, several of our employees enrolled in night classes use their lunch breaks for study time.

A tuition refund program is a benefit as well as an investment in our employees. It is just as critical as health insurance and vacation pay and is vital for the health of our employees and the future of our bank. A tuition refund program is a natural process in our TQM philosophy for striving for continuous improvement. I realize costs are always a factor, but consider the benefits: well trained, knowledgeable employees, an investment in our greatest asset.

Index